What Do We Know about God?

What Do We Know about God?

Evidence from the Hebrew Scriptures

MICHAEL J. LOWIS

Foreword by Albert Jewell

RESOURCE *Publications* · Eugene, Oregon

WHAT DO WE KNOW ABOUT GOD?
Evidence from the Hebrew Scriptures

Resource Publications
An Imprint of Wipf and Stock Publishers
199 W. 8th Ave., Suite 3
Eugene, OR 97401

www.wipfandstock.com

PAPERBACK ISBN: 978-1-5326-3359-1
HARDCOVER ISBN: 978-1-5326-3361-4
EBOOK ISBN: 978-1-5326-3360-7

Manufactured in the U.S.A.   JULY 24, 2017

Contents

Tables and Figures

Foreword

ANYONE ATTEMPTING TO WRITE a book on God is either very brave or rather foolhardy. However, Michael Lowis has not been daunted in this self-imposed task. What is required is a complex combination of qualifications: theologian, Bible scholar, inter-faith student, anthropologist, historian, philosopher and psychologist. Lowis appears to be well qualified across the board.

Writing as a Christian, he wisely restricts his study to the Hebrew scriptures which he takes as the basis for the two other Abrahamic 'religions of the book', Christianity and Islam. In so doing he displays an almost encyclopaedic knowledge of his subject and an awareness of what many traditional and modern scholars have to say. All Old Testament books are covered by means of an impressive examination of what they have to tell us of the attributes of God who emerges as a very real rather than shadowy figure.

The writer is not afraid to raise and address troubling issues such as the doubts as to the veracity of scriptures which evolved over many centuries necessarily raise or regarding how God may be expected to answer prayers without turning human beings into mere puppets.

Lowis writes primarily for two groups: those who are questioners when it comes to faith in God and Christians who wish to delve more deeply into the God they worship. After helpfully displaying the evidence he rightly leaves his readers to make their own minds up.

It is truly amazing what he manages to include in little more than a hundred pages!

Rev Dr Albert Jewell
Leeds
United Kingdom

Preface

GOD HAS BEEN AROUND for a long time—in fact from the very beginning—but what do we know about him? Perhaps this is a silly question, because the God of Judaism, Christianity, and Islam is regarded as unknowable. It does, however, require a lot of confidence to praise, worship, and thank something or someone that is unknowable. The faithful pray either silently or audibly, believing that their words will be heard and their pleas answered.

Imagine a conversation between a man who has been living in isolation (or was from another planet), and who has not received any teaching about God. He encounters a woman who is praying aloud. "Excuse me madam", the stranger says, "I don't see anyone else nearby. To whom are you talking?"

"I am praying to my God", replies the woman.

"But where is this God?"

"He is in heaven."

"Can we go there to meet him in person?"

"Heaven is not a place you can visit whilst you are still alive and on this earth, but we do hope to meet him in our next life one day."

"Alright, I don't really understand, but what sort of person is this God of yours?"

"He is invisible, but at the same time he is everywhere, all powerful, and he knows everything. Actually, we should not be using words like *he* and *him*, but we only continue to do so because the ancients started this convention, and they were very patriarchal."

"Hmm, I am still puzzled why you wish to communicate with someone who you can't see, and can't visit, yet seem to be convinced exists. What *do* you know about this God?"

"Well, there is quite a lot about him written in a book called *The Bible*, but it is often rather cryptic and needs some effort to interpret at times."

"That is very interesting, thank you. I would like to buy a copy of this book, and read about your God for myself." And with that, the stranger wanders off to find the nearest bookseller, in order to learn more about the Almighty.

Apologies for this rather simple little narrative, but it caused me to think just how I would respond if I were the one who was praying, and was questioned by someone who really had no understanding of what I was doing. If I was asked what God was like, what were his qualities and attributes, what did he do, and how do we know all this, just how would I respond?

This prompted me to undertake the task of trying to find out all I could about the nature and character of God, through a careful and detailed study of the Hebrew Scriptures (Old Testament). Of course, Christians will also turn to the New Testament, believing that Jesus Christ was the Son of God, and that Jesus spoke quite a lot about the one who he referred to as "Our Father in heaven." But this would not satisfy the Jews or Muslims, who acknowledge the older Scriptures, but do not accept that Jesus was the Son of God.

Thus, in order to be acceptable to adherents of each of the faiths that acknowledge Abraham as their founder, I decided to restrict my quest to the Hebrew Scriptures, except for a few occasions where a New Testament text clarifies a comment that appears in its older companion.

My intention throughout this exercise was to maintain an open mind and, where appropriate, be skeptical and even critical of what has been written in the Bible. Many otherwise religious people do not believe everything they are supposed to, and my own approach was to try to find convincing evidence, rather than just accept everything on faith. To help in this quest, many additional sources were consulted, and the views of other scholars and commentators were taken into account when reporting the findings. These are referenced within the text, and there is an extensive bibliography at the end of the book that can be used as a resource by those who may wish to undertake further study of this subject for themselves.

The exercise revealed an unanticipated amount of detail, and the findings form the main body of the present book. It should be emphasised, as I have done in this account, that this was not an attempt to anthropomorphize God by reducing his qualities down to the level that can be applied to mere mortals. Nevertheless, it may help one to know God, and feel closer to him, if we can use at least a few familiar "human" terms to describe some of his qualities.

The first chapters in this book review some of the earliest signs that could indicate religious beliefs, and these date back a surprisingly long time. Following from this, there are brief accounts of the origins and key beliefs of each of the five major world religions. Before embarking on an analysis of the Scriptures, factors that can influence the reliability of the texts are reviewed. Often some detailed exegesis is needed to uncover what was originally written, and under what circumstances. The next chapter summarizes the dates, authors, and main topics of each of the books in the Hebrew Scriptures that yielded pertinent information for this study.

How did the God of Abraham originate? Did he have a beginning? What is his name? These questions are debated in chapter 5, before the enquiry moves on to a discussion of the main attributes of God that are revealed in the Scriptures. Eight chapters then discuss the outcome of the search for evidence of what God does. These start, appropriately, with the topic of creation, including how the biblical account compares with the scientific view. Highly pertinent is the question: what was there right at the beginning? Miracles where the laws of nature appear to have been overridden are then reviewed, followed by the healing miracles. In both cases, scientific and medical advances may offer rational explanations for what really happened.

The presence of 613 laws in the Scriptures begs the question: how many of these came straight from God? The enquiry then moves on to how God judges and punishes sinners, but also rewards for the faithful. The first of the remaining two topics concerns the prophesies that a Messiah will come, some of which bear a remarkable resemblance to subsequent events in the life of Jesus. Finally, the discussion centers on the numerous references to prayer, and the confidence exhibited by many Scripture writers that they are both heard, and responded to.

The final chapter summarizes what the enquiry has revealed about the God of Abraham, before ending with a brief mention of two more intriguing questions. These are: has his audible voice ever been heard, and has anyone seen the personhood of God? There are indeed some clues regarding these issues in the Scriptures. It is concluded that, hopefully, this study has helped us to see God not as a just a remote entity, but instead has let us value him as a being with tangible characteristics and a personality. When we feel that we can anticipate the likes, dislikes, and responses of individuals, we can grow to know and trust them. Perhaps we can now be a little closer to regarding God in this way.

Michael J. Lowis
Northampton
United Kingdom

Acknowledgments

I AM INDEBTED TO Rev Dr Albert Jewell, Visiting Research Fellow of Glyndwr University, Wrexham, Wales, for not only kindly agreeing to write the Foreword to this book, but also for his many helpful suggestions. Without his keen eye, embarrassing errors would have gone undetected.

My grateful thanks are also extended to Dr Teresa A. Fisher, Professor, Bronx Community College, for her corrections during the proof-reading stage.

There have been others who have patiently tolerated my questions, fired at them without warning, when I have struggled with particular issues. Some are mentioned in the text, but I am grateful to them all for their help.

Introduction

THE ANSWERS TO THE very profound questions concerning how God began, what are his virtues, and what does he do, will depend very much on whether or not a person believes in a one, supreme, creator deity as portrayed in the holy texts of the Abrahamic religions. These comprise the major faiths of Judaism, Christianity, and Islam, along with the Baha'i that originated in Iran, and the Rastafarians that started in Jamaica. For these adherents, the opening words of the Hebrew Scriptures, known by Christians as the Old Testament, provide a hint: "In the beginning God created the heavens and the earth" (Genesis 1:1; all biblical quotations taken from the *New International Version*, NIV, Bible unless otherwise stated).

These words suggest that God already existed "in the beginning," presumably as a solitary entity, before the universe was created. The Gospel of John appears to confirm this with the passage: "In the beginning was the Word, and the Word was with God, and the Word was God" (John 1:1). Although this might be the best response a believer can offer about the origin of God, it still leaves us with a nagging feeling that the query has not been resolved. How, then, was God created? Can something be created out of nothing?

There are many religions in the world other than the Abrahamic group, and they often have their own varieties of god. Some are polytheistic, believing in more than one deity. For example, Jainism (in India) venerates five supreme beings, whilst Taoism (China) and Shintoism (Japan) each recognize multiple divine entities. Hinduism (India) has many male and female gods but, these are all generally regarded as being earthly manifestations of one chief god (see chapter 2). In addition, there are beliefs subsumed under the heading of earth religions. These include the worship of plants, animals, fertility gods, and other objects related to nature.

Being religious generally refers to adherence to the beliefs, practices and rituals of a traditional doctrine. Whilst this will usually imply those linked to a particular church denomination, strictly speaking the definition does not exclude devotion to a way of life, hobby, political party or other group that a person may hold dear. Spirituality is something different. It has been described as a way of being and experiencing that comes from the awareness of a transcendent dimension.[1] In turn, something that is transcendent is beyond or above the range of normal physical experience. Although there may be a significant overlap between the two, it is possible to have spiritual faith in a higher power whilst not necessarily being aligned to any orthodox religion.[2]

Those who have no feelings of spirituality, and do not acknowledge any deity or other object of worship, will be untroubled by the question of how God began. The idea that life originated according to evolutionary principles, and that human behavior developed in a way that helped to ensure the survival of the species, does not require the intervention of a divine being. Indeed, non-believers will maintain that we live in a secular world—there is no God, just people who are born, live a life largely of their own making, and then die.

The enquiry detailed in the pages to follow will try to answer such questions as:

---

1. Elkins et al., *Toward a Humanistic Phenomenological Spirituality*, 5–18.

2. MacDonald et al., *A Survey of Measures of Transpersonal Constructs*, 171–231.

What are the earliest indications of a belief in a transcendent dimension?

Why did religions, or spiritual beliefs, based on a supreme being originate?

When and how did the major religions of world come into being?

When did the God of Abraham first appear?

What do we know about the nature of the Abrahamic God?

What does the God of Judaism, Christianity, and Islam do?

Are there any benefits from having a belief in God?

To help with this quest, evidence uncovered by scientists, archaeologists, and anthropologists will be consulted, along with the views of theological scholars. In order to try and discover something about what God is like, clues will be sought from the most comprehensive and reliable text on this subject that is available. This is a book written by several authors, and it describes events that occurred as far back as 2,000 BC. The resource in question is the Hebrew Scriptures (Old Testament), regarded by Jews, Christians and Muslims as an authentic account of the history of their respective religions prior to the start of the Christian Era.

A superficial reading of these texts is unlikely to provide all the information that is contained within; it is sometimes allegorical, disguised, hidden, or even inaccurately reported or translated into our modern languages. In order to try and discover new knowledge and insights, a detailed 'reading between the lines' exegesis is needed. This involves a critical explanation or interpretation of the texts that includes comparing different versions and translations, in order to arrive as close as possible to what the original author intended.

Placing so much reliance on a text that is important to at least three major world religions, does not imply in any way that the present book has been written with the intention of trying to convert those who belong to other faiths, or none. The Scriptures are, if nothing else, a detailed account of certain events that occurred in ancient times. They can, therefore, be read as much for their historical content as for any deeper revelations they may hold for those who believe in the God of Abraham.

Note that, when dates are referred to in the chapters that follow, the designations BCE (Before the Christian Era) and CE (in the Christian Era) will be used, rather than BC and AD, in deference to those who do not subscribe the Christian religion. Also, we cannot always be sure of the precise dates for ancient events, so most of those cited should be regarded as only approximations.

Chapter 1 ௴

First Signs of Religious Beliefs

IT IS OF COURSE impossible to be certain when religious beliefs originated, or anything approaching religious practices were first enacted, but they could date from the very beginnings of hominid life on earth. Perhaps it all began with the veneration of the sun or moon or various aspects of nature that were held to be important in the cycle of birth, death and the food chain. G. van der Leeuw and C. J. Bleeker (1955),[1] speculated that primitive human beings had a mentality that did not involve logical thinking, but instead regarded everything as a potential object of religious veneration. He suggested that the concept of religion developed over time in three phases.

Firstly there was *dynamism*, the belief in powers or natural forces that control the world, and the desire to manipulate them. Although this capacity could be attached to objects such as a meteorite, or ceremonial staff, people could also bear special powers, for example priests, medicine men, or shamans. Secondly there was *animism*, a theory developed by E. B. Tylor in 1871.[2] He suggested that the early stages of religion stemmed from the concept of soul and spirits. Primitive man's explanation of dreams, breathing, and other mental and physical experiences convinced him of

1. *De Godsdiensten der Wereld*, 402.
2. In: Söderblom, *Das Werdeen des Gottesglaubens*, 11.

the existence of a soul that leaves the body after death. This idea was then projected onto plants and animals, and even inanimate objects in the environment, so that everything was thought to have a soul. According to Tylor, a belief in the existence of independent spirits then led to the notion that there were gods.

The third phase in the development of religion is the start of a belief in a creator—a supreme being. Heiler[3] refers to "causal god-concepts"—the theory that a deity was conceived to account for events and phenomena seen in the natural world. An example would be the appearance of comets in the sky, and the belief that these were sent by a god as signs to humanity. It was only a small step to see this deity as the creator, father, mother, or maker of the world, including of humankind.

An alternative explanation is known as the Way of Pre-eminence, meaning that the concept of a god was arrived at by adding together everything that is good and right, and attributing this to a deity.[4] Heiler suggests yet another possibility, called the Way of Denial. This idea holds that the divinity is so great that it is beyond human understanding, and can only be spoken about in a negative way. For example, he (or she) is invisible, inaudible, intangible, or a non-being.[5]

Whilst these three phases suggest the possible evolution of individual beliefs and the idea of a supreme being, the next developmental step would involve communal activities. Those persons who were thought to possess special powers, as mentioned in the *dynamism* phase, might lead the community in specific rituals. These could include making use of idols or objects considered sacred, or even conducting sacrifices to appease the gods of nature.

Probably the oldest object yet found that may have had some mystical significance is known as the Makapansgat Pebble from South Africa. It is about three million years old, and was discovered in a cave associated with the bones of the early hominid *Australopithacus africanus*. It is not fabricated, but natural wear

3. *Erscheinungsformen und Wesen der Religion* 455.
4. Ibid., 462.
5. Ibid., 467.

has created patterns on it that resemble a face (see Figure 1). It is believed that the stone was picked up some distance away and carried to where it was subsequently found. Thus it must have been held in some regard, although it is not known if it was kept just for the novelty of its facial appearance, or because it was believed to hold some mysterious powers.

Figure 1. The Makapansgat pebble
(Image in public domain)

The evidence from early burial practices may provide firmer grounds for the existence of religious or spiritual beliefs. For example, taking care to bury the dead in a ritualistic way, perhaps one that suggested preparing them for a passage to another realm or afterlife, may indicate belief in a transcendent power.

In an article published in 2009, Joshua Mark[6] stated that, in cultures such as Mesopotamia, tombs and graves were cut into the ground in the expectation that souls of the departed would more easily reach the afterlife, thought to exist underground. He added that such practices can be traced back to over 100,000 years ago. The earliest confirmed example of this is the Grave of Qafzeh in

6. *Burial Definition*

Israel, which is a group tomb of 15 people buried in a cave, along with their tools and other ritual artifacts.

Neanderthals existed alongside *Homo sapiens* for a time, until the former died out about 40,000 years ago. Although there may be even earlier evidence, Ker Than (2013)[7] gives details of a Neanderthal skeleton dating from about 50,000 BC, that was unearthed in southwestern France. Excavations indicated that the companions of the deceased took great care to dig the grave so as to protect the body from scavengers. Subsequently, 20 or so other sites have so far been uncovered throughout Western Europe, confirming similar burial practices. Ker Than concluded that such behavior shows that the Neanderthals were capable of symbolic thought. This links with other findings that indicate they probably decorated themselves with colored pigments, and jewelry made of feathers and shells.

Evidence of an early belief in some sort of transcendent dimension is not restricted to gravesites. John Roach (2003)[8] describes how, in 1939, a statue was discovered in Hohle Fels Cave in southwestern Germany. Known as the Lowenmensch (Lion-man) figurine, it is carved out of woolly mammoth ivory and measures nearly a foot in length. It is believed to have been fabricated about 30,000 years ago. What makes this object so interesting is that it is anthropomorphic, meaning that it gives human characteristics to an animal. Could this little statue have played a significant role in the mythology of early humans, perhaps even having religious connotations? Roach cites experts who think it may either represent admiration for the powerful, fast and aggressive lion, or provide evidence of shamanism—a device to help interaction with the spirit world.

What may be one of the oldest human-made sites of religious worship—the world's first temple—was discovered a few miles from the city of Sanliurfa, in the southeast of Turkey. According to the official website,[9] it is known as Gobeklitepe, and is believed to

7. *Neanderthal Burials*
8. *Ancient Figurines Found—From First Modern Humans?*
9. Anonymous, *http://gobeklitepe.info*

be about 12,000 years old. This date places the time of construction in the Neolithic A period, a time before pottery, metallurgy, writing, or the wheel. The site comprises a series of mainly circular and oval-shaped structures set on top of a hill. Within the temple there is a series of T-shaped stone pillars, many of which are decorated with carvings of abstract symbols, along with depictions of animals including foxes, snakes, and lion. Some of the stone structures weigh as much as 20 tons, and the only tools available for dressing and carving them were pointed flints. It is speculated that a priestly cast oversaw the construction of the temple, and that it was a place of pilgrimage and worship.

It would be difficult to deny that the ancient Egyptians brought a level of sophistication to tomb building and burial practices that it would be hard to beat even today. Joshua Mark (2016)[10] states that depictions of gods and the afterlife first appeared on the walls of Egyptian tombs, about 6,000 years ago. The Step Pyramid of Djoser at Saqqara is the earliest monument of its type to be constructed, and it dates from circa 2650–2575 BCE. Egyptian religion held that life on earth was only part of our total existence, and that it continued after our earthly death, provided we had complied with certain requirements. Elaborate embalming procedures were intended to preserve the body for its passage to, and life in, the next world.

A range of deities was acknowledged, and it was believed that these beings were in control of the elements and forces of nature. They include Ra the sun god, Amun the creator god, and Isis the mother goddess. Formal religious practices were controlled by the pharaoh, who was believed to possess divine power; he or she also acted as an intermediary between the people and the gods.

The few examples of early religious beliefs and practices outlined above are just some of the many that have been discovered by archaeologists and anthropologists. Why is it that, as far back as it is possible to determine, the evidence points to a widespread belief in the existence of a higher force or entity? One answer is

10. *Ancient Egyptian Religion*

that the God that we acknowledge today was at work in the heart and minds of people from the very beginning.

For those who do not believe in such a being, there are alternative explanations. These are often based on the desire to avoid what psychologists call Cognitive Dissonance. We seek to avoid being troubled by things that we cannot readily explain, and this may lead us to resolve these inner conflicts by concocting solutions that may appear fanciful to an observer. Being able to accept that some religious force was at work would eliminate the need to seek logical explanations for the workings of nature, and avoid the dissonance that could result from simply not knowing.

More recently, researchers have claimed that brain scans reveal significant differences in neural activity between religious and non-religious people. Sam Harris[11] conducted trials that imaged the area known as the ventromedial prefrontal cortex, a region of the brain involved in emotional judgment, processing uncertainty, assessing rewards, and thinking about oneself. He states that the results showed a wide range of signal differences that he attributed to the level of religiosity of the participants. Some investigators have even claimed there is a specific God Spot in the brain that makes people susceptible to religious and mystical experiences.

If findings like these are valid, does this mean that those who claim to be religious are merely responding to electrical activity in a particular part of the brain that they have, but others do not? Even if this were the case, it would not preclude the God Spot being planted there by God himself, assuming he or she exists. It would, however, be wise to treat such evidence from brain scans with a degree of reservation, regardless of any wish to discover physiological explanations for religious experiences.

These experiments are notoriously hard to replicate, and the results are far less conclusive than researchers may think. It is difficult to conduct any research in an unbiased way, and investigators who claim significant outcomes may fall into the trap of grasping at any result that appears to confirm their previously held view.

---

11. In: Butler-Bowdon, 50 *Philosophy Classics*

Does the evidence so far discussed indicate that the notion of God is simply a delusion to explain the otherwise unexplainable, and avoid cognitive dissonance? It is no coincidence that *The God Delusion* is the title of a book by Richard Dawkins (2006), in which he attacks all aspects of a supernatural God. To add to such negative views, below are some quotations from well-known atheists, starting with one from Dawkins himself.

i) "I doubt that religion can survive deep understanding . . . faith is the great cop out, the great excuse to avoid the need to think and evaluate evidence." (Richard Dawkins, 1941—)

ii) "I say quite deliberately that the Christian religion as organized by its churches has been and still is the principle enemy of moral progress in the world." (Bertrand Russell, (1872–1970)

iii) "Religion is excellent stuff for keeping common people quiet." (Napoleon Bonaparte, 1769–1821)

iv) "When I think of all the harm the Bible has done, I despair of writing anything to equal it." (Oscar Wilde, 1854–1900)

v) "When a man is freed of religion he has a better chance to live a normal and wholesome life." (Sigmund Freud, 1856–1939)

vi) "Religion is the sign of the oppressed creature, the heart of a heartless world, just as it is the spirit of a spiritless situation. It is the opium of the people." (Karl Marx, 1818–1883)

Most of what follows in this book concerns firstly an exploration of the origins of a belief in the existence of God as an entity. This is attempted by looking at how some of the world's major religions developed. Then, in more detail, it describes an investigation into what we can learn about the Abrahamic God, through careful analysis of the Hebrew Scriptures. These often contain descriptions of the qualities that the prophets attributed to their creator, omnipotent God.

To end this current chapter, however, it will be useful to review the main arguments for and against the existence of God as the Supreme Being. These were succinctly summarized by John Hick.[12] Firstly, here is his case *against* the belief in God:

i) The gods whom people worship are imaginary beings, unconsciously fabricated by society to exercise control over the thoughts and behaviours of the individual: our society binds us together, and supports us in times of crisis (the Social Theory).

ii) Religious beliefs are illusions, wish fulfillments, mental defenses against threats, and a psychological crutch—an obsessional neurosis that is left behind when we rely on scientific knowledge (the Freudian Theory).

iii) If God is perfectly loving, he must wish to abolish evil; if he is all-powerful, he must be able to do it. But evil exists, therefore God cannot be both omnipotent and perfectly loving (the Problem of Evil Argument).

iv) Scientific information has steadily expanded, especially since the Renaissance, and many of the assertions made in the Bible have been countered by scientific discoveries, for example the creation of the world and humankind, healings and other alleged miracles. As scientific knowledge continues to expand, so the mysteries of religion will decrease and nature can be studied without any reference to God (the Challenge of Science Argument).

We now need to orient ourselves toward the task of learning what we can about the origin and nature of the God acknowledged by Jews, Christians, and Muslims, which comprises the major portion of the present book. In order to do this, it is necessary to make the a priori assumption that such an entity does exist, otherwise it would be a pointless exercise. To help us achieve this, here are Hick's arguments *supporting* the belief in God:

i) As revealed by the unfolding of God's revelation of Himself, there must exist an independent and supremely perfect being

12. *Arguments for the Existence of God*

that is God, for a God without existence would not be God (the Ontological Argument—the science that deals with the nature of things).

ii) Everything that happens has a cause. Tracing this back, there must have been a first cause that was not dependent on anything else: that was God (the First Cause or Cosmological Argument).

iii) The natural world is complex. Just as a watch cannot exist without a designer, so the natural world could not have come about without a designer: that was God (the Design or Teleological Argument).

iv) The existence of human beings' religious (that is, belief in a personal deity), moral and aesthetic experiences are cumulative and point to God (the Theistic Argument).

v) Moral values are not capable of naturalistic explanation in terms of human needs and desires—there must be a trans-human source (that is, God) for the basis of these values (the Moral Argument).

vi) Miracles, answers to prayers, inner voices, mystical and ecstatic experiences, visions and revelations, are convincing proofs of the existence of God, but need to be experienced personally (the Special Events and Experiences Argument).

One of the limitations of Hick's points, both for and against the existence of God, is that most of them are based on logical arguments. Whilst these might seem to be rational, they can be countered in an equally logical way. For example, the Problem of Evil Argument can be defended by stating that we have been given free will by a God who did not want to be all-controlling. Likewise, it does not follow that the complex natural world had to have a designer; natural selection can account for it. Perhaps the most meaningful of Hick's statements is the last in his list: in order to be convinced of God's existence, it needs to be experienced personally. The prophets who will be quoted in later chapters would no doubt have been convinced that God had indeed spoken to them.

Chapter 2 ⌒∿

Origins of the Major Religions

How many religions are there in the world today? There are so many variants that it is almost impossible to be sure, but one website lists 79 of them[1]. Most can be broadly categorized as belonging to either a Middle Eastern group that would embrace Judaism, Christianity and Islam, or a Far Eastern one that includes the Chinese faiths and those of India such as Hinduism and Buddhism. It would serve little purpose to discuss each of the sects here, and it would also be very boring. The subject matter of this chapter will, therefore, be concentrated on just five of the oldest and largest world religions still practiced today.

Their names, possible dates of origin, and numbers of adherents are as follows:

i) Hinduism (the precursor appeared c 2,500 BCE) (900 million)

ii) Judaism (Abraham enters Canaan c 2,000 BCE) (14 million)

iii) Buddhism (Gautama Buddha died c 480 BCE) (376 million)

iv) Christianity (Jesus probably died 33 CE) (2.1 billion)

v) Islam (Muhammad died 632 CE) (1.3 billion)

(Dates from: Zaehner[2]).

1. Anonymous, *http://www.humanreligions.info/religions.html*
2. *The Concise Encyclopedia of Living Faiths*

Of these five religions three, Christianity, Judaism, and Islam are monotheistic. They each acknowledge the God of the Hebrew Scriptures, and are therefore sometimes referred to as the Abrahamic Religions. There are variants of Hinduism but most are polytheistic, and follow their own version of God. Buddhism is not a theistic religion, but is a life-code designed to eliminate the causes of human suffering, and attain perfect enlightenment. Delving into how these religions started should help us to understand how the concept of God originated.

HINDUISM

Unlike most of the other major religions, Hinduism had no single founder and no specific date of origin. Although there are regional variations, it can be described as an Indian belief system based on a complex arrangement of faith and practice. This includes the notion of transmigration—that the soul inhabits many bodies until it reaches its final goal. All animals and plants are believed to possess a soul, and the level in which a re-birth takes place is determined by *karma*, or the effect of deeds carried out during the previous life.[3]

Basham notes that the earliest civilization in India, dating back 2,000 years before the birth of Christ, practiced a religion that was in some ways similar to that of later Hinduism. These people worshiped a mother goddess, and also acknowledged male divinities, along with sacred animals and plants. About 500 years later, their land was invaded by the Ārya people, who had a priestly cast, worshiped several male deities, and conducted sacrifices. They also composed hymns, firstly preserved by oral traditions and later written down in the sacred book *Rig Veda*. Perhaps around 500 BCE, new doctrines appeared, including the notion of transmigration.

In order to try and escape from this eternal cycle of death and re-birth, some men decided to take to a life of severe asceticism,

---

3. Basham, in Zaehner, *The Concise Encyclopaedia of Living Faiths*, 217.

meditation, and even self-mortification. They claimed to have discovered systems that led straight to the ultimate truth and full salvation. New texts were written—the *Upanishads*—that emphasized the unity of the individual soul with the absolute 'World-Soul'. The basic tenant of unity remains a key doctrine of Hinduism today, along with the necessity of fully realizing this in order to escape from the birth-death cycle and achieve the highest bliss in which personality is lost. As put so poetically by Geoffrey Parrinder,[4] the mortal becomes immortal and, like a river entering the sea and losing its identity, the wise man goes to the divine being.

Further developments in the Hindu religion occurred as the end of the pre-Christian era approached. Sacrifices became less popular, and the new deities Vishnu and Śiva came to the fore, along with Brahma who is described as "the personified word through which creation came into being."[5] Many gods were added later, including Ganesha (with the elephant's head), Parvati (with many arms), Krishna, Hanuman, Durga, and Lakshmi. Paradoxically, many regard Hinduism as being monotheistic, because the followers believe that all these deities are manifestations of the same god or divine energy, who is without form. All are free to worship which of these representations they like best.

On the matter of creation, Hindus believe that original existence comprised just a primal *thing*, which was self-maintaining and autonomous. Then, in this thing, a desire (Kāma) arose, and also a consciousness. This led to a division that triggered the beginning of a process that led to the existence of the gods, and to creation. At least some of these gods had a specific role. For example, Varuna was creator of the sun and earth, Mitra was the benevolent god of the day-sky, Indra was the god of raw power, Rudra the leader of the wild storm winds, and Sūryá was the sun goddess.[6]

The Hindus regarded the universe as being immensely large and ancient, long before other religions and scientists did. Until

4. *Asian Religions*, 41.
5. Ringgren & Strom, *Religions of Mankind*, 345.
6. Ibid., 312.

comparatively recently, most other people believed that the cosmos was relatively small in size, that it was created not very long ago, and that the earth was at the centre of the universe. Hindu adherents also acknowledge a creator god—usually Brahma, as mentioned above—just as the Abrahamic religions hold that their God made all things.

Geoffrey Parrinder[7] notes that the impersonal teaching of the Upanishads is being replaced with the belief in a personal god, and that individual devotion often centres on one of the two main gods Vishnu or Śiva, but it can also be on any of the many other manifestations.

A key text for the Hindus is the *Bhagavad-Gita* ("The song of the Lord"). Its origin is difficult to date, with estimates ranging from about 500 years before the birth of Christ, to 100 years after. The authorship is attributed to the Sage Vyasa, and it comprises a dialogue between a warrior, Arjuna, and Lord Krishna. Scholars claim there are some parallels between the lives of Krishna and Jesus, and between the *Gita* and the Sermon on the Mount.[8]

Included in the words of wisdom contained in the *Gita* is the statement that the single, central fact of the cosmology is called Brahman—the Reality, the total Godhead. When it is considered that Brahman is lodged within an individual, it is called the Atman. In fact, the Atman resides within everything, living or dead. The power of the Brahman is the basis of all mind and matter—it causes all existence to come into being.

In addition to such philosophy there is dilemma of Arjuna who, although a warrior and commander, does not want to fight in a battle where his kinsmen will be killed. Krishna, who has taken the role of Arjuna's charioteer, reminds him that, in the absolute sense, there is no such act as killing. The Atman, the indwelling Godhead, is the only reality. The body is simply an appearance; its destruction is an illusion, as the soul (Atman) moves to another body after death. Krishna tells Arjuna that he should prefer to die doing his duty. The *Gita* neither sanctions nor condemns war.

7. *Asian Religions*, 45.
8. Prabhavananda & Isherwood, *Bhagavad-Gita*, 28–9.

To summarise, Hinduism is an ancient religion that has evolved and changed over time. The religion has many gods, but they are all believed to be earthly manifestations of the same supreme divinity. It may be inferred that the idea of the gods originated to account for the creation of the universe, and various other aspects of nature such as the sun, or storms. There are some interesting parallels between this religion and Christianity, for example Krishna and Jesus.

JUDAISM

The difficulty in discussing the date of origin for Judaism lies in deciding what to use as a starting point. The oldest books of the Hebrew Scriptures, the Pentateuch, are generally believed to have been written by Moses around 1,440 BCE, but some scholars date them 100 years later, or even that they were compiled from various sources during the first millennium BCE. Events are related that occurred around 2,000 BCE, the accounts of which were previously preserved through oral tradition. If we take the biblical accounts literally, then the timeline stretches back much further. Donald Joyner[9] states that the creation of all things, as recorded in the book Genesis, occurred in the year 3761 BCE. This is the date that the Jewish people believe God made Adam.

A slightly earlier date was calculated by Irish Archbishop James Ussher (1581–1656). He computed the chronologies contained in Genesis chapters 5 and 11, together with clues from other biblical passages, and arrived at the year 4004 BCE as the date of creation. Until comparatively recently, this was widely accepted by the Christian community, and Ussher's chronology is sometimes included in the margins of some of the older King James Bibles.

An alternative approach to identifying the origins of Judaism is to determine when adherents of the ancient religions of Canaan and Babylon came together and adopted a common theology embracing monotheism, divine law, election, and the Covenant. The

9. *The Twelfth Journey*, 15.

Hebrew kingdom emerged in Canaan, from what were previously scattered Israelite tribes, under the first king: Saul (1043–1011 BCE). Jewish religion continued to evolve, experiencing many defining moments that served to mould it into the format that is practiced today. To highlight just one of these, Ringgren and Ström[10] mention the destruction of Jerusalem and its temple, followed by the period of Babylonian exile (586–538 BCE). During this time there was a strengthening of the doctrine and ethics of the religion, at the expense of the previous rituals and practices.

Although we have no precise date for the origins of Judaism, for the purposes of the present enquiry it will be assumed to be about 2000 BCE. This has been suggested as the time when Abraham (or Abram, as he was initially called) received a message from God telling him to journey form his home in Ur, Mesopotamia, to the land Canaan where he would found a great nation (Genesis, 12:1). However, some scholars have computed different dates for this. For example, Matt McClellan (2013)[11] carried out a detailed review of the history of Mesopotamia, and concluded that the patriarch must have lived during the Early Dynastic Period (2900–2350 BCE). Others have suggested that Abraham's journey was more recent: perhaps sometime between the nineteenth and sixteenth centuries before Christ.[12]

The geographical area that was Canaan, roughly corresponding to present day Lebanon, Syria, Jordan and Israel, has been occupied for a very long time. Evidence of prehistoric habitation dates back two or three hundred-thousand years. Modern humans have lived there since at least 9000 BCE, when they founded a permanent settlement that would become known as Jericho, one of the world's oldest cities. According to Michael Grant,[13] the first wave of Semitic-speaking peoples immigrated into the area from the Arabian Desert some time during the fourth pre-Christian millennium. They also spread into Mesopotamia and Egypt.

10. *Religions of Mankind*, 295.

11. *Abraham and the Chronology of Ancient Mesopotamia*

12. Grant, *The History of Ancient Israel*, 30.

13. Ibid., 9.

The Canaanites were already religious people prior to Abraham's visit. They were polytheistic, with many minor deities who could be approached, and to whom ordinary folk could attach themselves for protection. In addition, there were higher gods with more universal powers, which suggests there was a divine division of labour. Whilst this was very different to the monotheistic theology of the later Israelites, it nevertheless exercised a great influence on the latter, both positively and negatively.

The leading deities often appeared in Israel, for example El, the Mighty One, along with his son Baal. Baal's consort was Asherah, a tree goddess, and the Canaanites also revered Shemesh the sun-god and Yerah the moon-god. This veneration of deities associated with nature is only to be expected in a community relying on the fruitfulness of the earth, plants and flocks for their survival.

The offering of sacrifices was a common way that the people contacted their deities, as it was believed that the gods lived off the smell of the offerings. In times of major emergencies, however, the surest way to appease the divine power was to offer a human sacrifice; this may be a son, daughter or baby. Unfortunately, this practice lingered on even at the time of the kings of Judah, some two hundred years later.[14]

Jacob was Abraham's grandson, and he was given the name Israel by God because of his persistent loyalty. He is regarded as the founder of the Hebrew nation[15] which, for those who wish to use this as a yardstick, would advance the date of Judaism's origin by about 50 years. Jacob had 12 sons, who ultimately became leaders of the 12 tribes of Israel.

In summary, like Hinduism, Judaism is a religion with a very long history. There are also similarities between the polytheism of Hinduism and the range of deities acknowledged by the Canaanites, some of which, at least initially, influenced the emerging Judaism. The main differences between the two faiths are that Judaism did have an identifiable founder, and it did ultimately become monotheistic. In fact, Deuteronomy (6:4) is taken literally: "Hear,

14. Ibid., 22–5.
15. Joyner, *The Twelfth Journey*, 58.

O Israel: the Lord our God, the Lord is one." There is no triune God in Jewish doctrine. Abraham is regarded as a father figure, the embodiment of the principles of faith and obedience, and the first man to renounce idolatry, and recognize one God. He was thus not only the founder of Judaism, but of Christianity and Islam as well.

BUDDHISM

Buddhism will not be covered in any detail, but is included for the sake of completeness because of its ancient origins and the fact that it has many followers. It is not a true religion, in the sense that it acknowledges a god or other supreme being. Rather, it is a religion because it advocates a way of life that influences all or most of a person's daily activities, and is passionately followed by devoted adherents. Some of the rituals and practices come close to those carried out by followers of a theistic faith—the only difference being that these are not done to worship a deity or carry out any commands issued by such a being.

Buddhism does have a founder, and a reasonably accurate starting point. Siddhattha Gautama (or Gotama) the Buddha was born about 560 BCE in the city of Kapilavastu in the north east of India. At the age of 29 he decided to search for a meaningful existence, and went to live the life of an ascetic, but later abandoned this as it gave him no satisfaction. The story goes that he sat down under a sacred Bodhi (fig) tree, and experienced a spiritual awakening. Now he was an enlightened one—a Buddha. He thought that all the world's pain was the result of people's craving for life. If this craving can be forgotten, a person can enter the stage of eternal bliss—Nirvana. Buddha then devoted the rest of his life to spreading his message, and he died aged about 80 years.[16]

Although deities play no part in Buddhist practices today, gods have been mentioned in some accounts of the founder's life. For example, Parrinder[17] mentions Buddha's struggle with the evil

16. Ringgren & Ström, *Religions of Mankind*, 363.
17. *Asian Religions*, 67.

one Mara, and that "all the gods shouted with joy" when Gautama was victorious. Even the god Brahma, as venerated by the Hindus, apparently spoke with Buddha.

Buddhist doctrine is underpinned by four truths that relate to suffering, its cause, and the way of eliminating it. Freedom from suffering comes from following the Eightfold Path. These stages are made up of three clusters. Firstly there is enlightenment (from having the right view and resolve), secondly morality (ethical conduct involving the right speech, activity, and livelihood) and, thirdly, mind-training, or meditation (right endeavor, mindfulness, and concentration.[18]

Ringgren and Ström[19] emphasize the difficulty of being sure of many of the facts surrounding Buddhism, because the first accounts were only written down in the first or second century of the Christian era. Thus, the oral tradition that preserved Gautama's teachings for 600 or more years may have been corrupted with legend and romance before they were documented. Of course Buddhism is not unique in this regard, as we have already seen from the history of both Hinduism and Judaism.

CHRISTIANITY

Christianity shared its early history with Judaism, but it then became a separate religion for those who accepted Jesus Christ as the Messiah—the Son of God. What date to put on this is somewhat arbitrary. Jesus probably died in the year 33 CE, and the first mention of his followers by their generic name occurs in Acts (11:13). Verse 26 reads: " . . . Barnabas and Saul . . . taught great numbers of people. The disciples were called Christians first at Antioch." This New Testament book was believed to have been written by Luke, at a date somewhere between about 60 and 90 CE.

Historical accounts indicate that the early followers of Christ were Jews who continued to worship in synagogues. The divisions

18. Ibid., 72.
19. Ringgren & Ström, *Religions of Mankind*, 363.

between those who accepted the teachings of Jesus, and those who did not, gradually widened, especially after the destruction of the Jerusalem Temple in 70 CE. The Christians were forced out of the synagogues and into house groups, often meeting in secrecy to avoid persecution.

Some might prefer the date of 312 CE for the formal birth of Christianity, as this was when Emperor Constantine embraced the religion and ordered his troops to decorate their shields with appropriate symbols. In the following year, he officially legalized Christian worship.

A significant difference between Christianity and the other Abrahamic religions is in its belief in a triune God. Paul, in his First Letter to the Corinthians, separately mentions God the Father and the Lord Jesus Christ (8:6), and later adds the Holy Spirit (12:3). In his second Letter, he brings all three together in the well-known Christian benediction: "May the grace of the Lord Jesus Christ, and the love of God, and the fellowship of the Holy Spirit, be with you all." (13:14).

Because we shall be concentrating on the Hebrew Scriptures (Old Testament) texts for most of this investigation, there is little need for further details on the New Testament story. An exception will be when Jesus himself clarifies what was written in the older Scriptures, and these will be mentioned where appropriate.

ISLAM

This is the youngest of the religions being discussed here. It was founded by the Prophet Muhammad who was born in Mecca, in what is now Saudi Arabia, in about 570 CE and died in 632 CE. Mecca was already a town of pilgrimage, as visitors came to see the Kabah building that was believed to have been constructed by Abraham.[20] The religious milieu in the region included the cults of the moon-god and sun-goddess, inherited from the southern regions of the country. The northern regions worshipped the

20. Parrinder, *Asian Religions*, 5–20

supreme deity Allāh (akin to the Semitic El, see Judaism, above), his three daughters, and other gods.[21]

The story goes that, when Muhammad was aged 40, he was visited by the angel Gabriel, who told him that he was a prophet of God, and that he must proclaim the worship of one God (Allāh). Polytheism and idol worship must be outlawed. For this reason, Muslims today, as do the Jews, reject the idea of a triune God. Islam holds that Allāh is genderless, and has no partners or offspring.

Gabriel is said to have recited the whole of the Quran (or Koran), but Muhammad could neither read nor write, so he passed on the words from memory to others. After the prophet's death, the revelations were collected from oral tradition and written fragments by his companion Zayd, although it is believed that the Quran used today has been subjected to extensive redaction and revision. Muslims acknowledge the prophets of the Hebrew Scriptures, and regard Jesus as one of the greatest of God's messengers. Muhammad himself denied any suggestion of a supernatural character. He is held by his followers as being the last and greatest apostle of God.[22]

The basic doctrines of Islam (the Five Pillars of Faith) are concerned with prayer, fasting, almsgiving, pilgrimage, and profession of faith. The Quran also teaches that all our actions are predestined, with statements such as: "God guides who he wills and turns astray who he wills."[23] There is, however, some tension here as Muhammad himself attempted to win men to obedience to Allāh and, in so doing, recognized that there was freedom to accept or reject this. This has led to differences among Islamic sects regarding the doctrine of predestination, but a mid-tenth century compromise stated: "God determines man's destiny, but then man has the freedom to make that destiny his own."[24]

---

21. McCasland & Cairns, *Religions of the World*, 212.

22. Gibb, *Islam*, 166–99.

23. Ibid., 166–99.

24. Ringgren and Ström, *The Religions of Mankind*, 188; 193.

Chapter 3 ∾

Reliability of the Hebrew Scriptures

No ORIGINAL MANUSCRIPTS (AUTOGRAPHS) for any of the books of the Bible have ever been found. Even the most ancient texts are copies, sometimes several times over, with opportunities for errors, additions, omissions or redaction at every stage. Translators are also faced with the difficulty of preserving the precise, original meaning of words. The earliest narratives would have been written from a personal point of view, during a specific time in history, and in particular circumstances (the *Sitz im Leben*). It thus remains a challenge for exegetical scholars to firstly identify what the original writer actually wrote and, secondly, to establish the author's intended meaning.

There is yet a third task, for those who wish to take the research to its logical endpoint: that of interpretation. In other words, what does the message mean to us today? This combined investigative procedure is referred to as 'hermeneutics'. Throughout this exercise, a researcher has to try and suppress his or her own presuppositions and biases—not always an easy thing to do.

Further challenges remain for the scholar. Whereas some of the Bible texts were written as factual narratives, to be regarded as historical accounts of what had occurred, some were not. Stories were sometimes created that are etiological (to explain causes or origins), allegorical (to convey hidden meanings or imagery), or apocryphal (probably untrue, but typical of what could be true). Throughout history there have been differences of opinion on whether the biblical narratives should be taken literally, or be regarded as allegories with hidden meanings. These diverse views fall into two major camps, and their origins can be traced back respectively to the cities of Alexandria and Antioch.

Alexandria was founded by Alexander the Great and, from 330 BCE, it was the capital of Egypt. The Alexandrian scholars were inspired by Plato, who presented the world as a shadow of reality, differing from what is experienced by the human senses. They were also influenced by the Stoics who held that messages encoded in the Scriptures were coherent, rational, and accessible through non-literal interpretation.[1]

Sometime later, Pope Clement (c 150–215 CE) opined that the truth of the Scripture comes through a veil, and needs interpretation. It is therefore necessary to look beyond the letters to hear the voice behind the literal text.[2] Clement was the first Christian to justify and explain the meaning of the allegorical method, and he maintained that true meaning of the text was hidden from the Common Man.[3]

By contrast, early supporters of a literal meaning of the texts came from the city of Antioch, sited in Syria, some 20 miles inland. It was founded by the Macedonian King Seleucus Nicator, in about 300 BCE. One of the most significant practitioners of the Antiochene School was Theodore of Mopsuestia (c 350–428 CE), who criticized the Alexandrian allegorical methodology. He advocated the practice of plain meaning, declaring that no text can imitate something other than what it openly says, although it may be by figure of speech.[4]

John Chrysostom (c 347–407) was a priest at Antioch, and a friend of Theodore. He believed that God had to speak to humans in their language, with all its limitations (McKim, 1998). Whereas

1. Stallard, *Literary interpretation*, 14–55.

2. McKim, *Historical Handbook of Major Interpreters*.

3. Dockery, *The History of pre-critical biblical interpretation*, 1–30.

4. Norris, *Antiochene Interpretation*, 29–32.

the Alexandrian School based its exegesis on Plato's rather other-worldly view, the Antiochenes preferred to follow the more down-to-earth philosophy of Aristotle.[5]

Today, holders of these apparently opposing views can be regarded as being in either the conservative or the liberal inter-pretative camp. The former, include hyper-Fundamentalists and Evangelicals, although there are also those with more moderate stances. Their argument is determined by the extent to which the texts are regarded as the actual words of God, as compared with them being those of mortal humans who were divinely inspired to a greater or lesser extent. If the former, then what was written becomes a matter of fact and indisputable, with absolute authority. As a consequence, they say that a passage can be lifted from the scriptures and applied to a particular situation today.

One of the supporters of this view is James Hamilton, who states unequivocally that, "The . . . books of the Protestant canon are inspired by the Holy Spirit and therefore inerrant and totally trustworthy."[6] To support this, he cites a number of Bible passages including 2 Tim (3:16): "All scripture is God breathed," and 2 Pet (1:20–21): "No prophecy of Scripture came about by the prophet's own interpretation . . . but prophets, though human, spoke from God as they were carried along by the Holy Spirit."

References from the Hebrew Scriptures also support the con-servative approach, including: "The tablets [that Moses brought down from the mountain] were the work of God; the writing was the writing of God" (Ex 32:16), and "Every word of God is flaw-less" (Prov 30:5). There are also examples of the audible voice of God. These include: "As the sound of the trumpet grew louder and louder, Moses spoke and the voice of God answered him." (Ex 19:19). From the New Testament we have, "a voice from the cloud said 'This is my Son, whom I love'" (Mat 17:5). From this and other evidence, Hamilton concludes that the Bible is self-authenticating . . . "we believe what it says . . . pure, perfect, inspired, and true."[7]

5. Dockery, *The History of pre-critical biblical interpretation*, 1–30.

6. *Still Sola Scripture*, 217.

7. Ibid, 236.

Those who subscribe to the opposite, liberal, viewpoint tend to regard the Bible as basically an account of the religious experiences of the authors, rather than words directly attributed to God and the Holy Spirit.[8] Extreme liberals take this further, see everything as subjective, and read whatever they wish into the Bible. Erickson[9] would regard this as Intuition Theory, which holds that the inspiration of the Scripture writers is no different from that of other great religious and philosophical thinkers, without the need for any divine involvement.

Postmodernism originated in the 1960s and 70s as a reaction to the previous modernist views of scientific objectivity. Followers of this philosophy believe that there is no ultimate truth, and that all that is perceived is subjective. Scripture is regarded as narrative, without propositional truths, but with inspiration that invites a personal response. McQuilkin[10] comments that postmodernism has directed us to examine more carefully our claims to infallible interpretations of the Bible.

Is there any way that these diverse approaches can be reconciled? The answer will be influenced by whether or not a person believes in the deity who is the subject of this discussion. Objective proof that God exists, especially for the skeptic, is likely to remain elusive, as belief usually comes through some sort of personal revelation or conviction that would defy scientific explanation. One thing is sure: God did not speak or write *any* of the words in the Bible in the languages in which they are now reported. As mentioned earlier, we remain at the mercy of the original eye witnesses, scribes and copyists, with the opportunities for errors at every stage. Do we have the confidence to follow the words of the unknown author of the Letter to the Hebrews, who wrote, "Now faith is the confidence in what we hope for and assurance about what we do not see." (11:1)?

Despite the many opportunities for scribing errors, there is reason to believe that the text of the Hebrew Scriptures has

8. McQuilkin, *Understanding and Applying the Bible*, 33–4.

9. *Christian Theology*, 206.

10. McQuilkin, *Understanding and Applying the Bible*, 57.

survived reasonably unscathed for a very long time. In about 250 BCE, the Hebrew texts available at that time were translated into Greek by about 70 Jewish scholars. This is called the *Septuagint* (Latin for 70), sometimes abbreviated to LXX.

There is another translation, known as the *Masoretic Text* (MT). This was complied over a period of time, stretching from the seventh to the tenth centuries CE, by a group of Masorite Jews who compared all known manuscripts. Although this is a more recent version than the LXX, it is the one most used for Protestant and some Catholic Bibles. The NIV Bible, published in 2011, contains the statement "For the Old Testament . . . the Masoretic Text . . . has been used throughout" (p. xiii), and the *Good News Bible* has a similar declaration.

Some assurance with regard to the reliability of the copying and editing can be gained from the fact that, although the LXX translation predates the MT by hundreds of years, the Hebrew Scriptures that have been identified in the Dead Sea Scrolls found at Qumran mostly confirm the MT version. Despite this, the Scripture quotations spoken by Jesus, Paul and others as cited in the New Testament are generally taken from the earlier LXX. Both these translations will be consulted in the present enquiry, in an effort to gain the best possible understanding of the text.

Although Malachi is the final book of the Scriptures, this is not to say that the Jewish people then stopped recording their history. To be included in the collection of books, the writings had to be accepted as being inspired by God.[11] In practice, this would mean that the texts were written by a prophet who had received messages from, or communicated with, the one God. Where there was doubt, the manuscripts were confined to the Jewish Apocrypha. The Mishnah (commentaries), and Talmud (oral law handed down from Moses) were written during the intertestamental period.

The major topic of the present book concerns what we can learn about the origin and nature of the Abrahamic God. This begs the question: do the Scriptures reveal anything about this?

---

11. Joyner, *The Twelfth Journey*, 67.

Erickson[12] distinguishes between revelation—God revealing himself directly to an individual, and inspiration—the influence of the Holy Spirit upon the Scripture writers, so that they are able to convey an accurate record of the revelation. This does not imply divine dictation; the choice of words will be left to the writer. Is this the intention of the statement in the Letter to Timothy that the Scripture is God breathed? (Vide supra).

It is the task of exegesis to try and tease out the intended meaning although, as McCartney and Clayton[13] state, interpretation is never value free; the Bible instructs us on ethics and truth. Deciding just what is right or wrong is an ethical act performed by the reader. It is perhaps little wonder why there are so many diverse views on what the Bible teaches us, and why so many writers have put pen to paper to create study guides and commentaries on the biblical texts.

The guiding principle that will be adopted during the present enquiry is that the Scriptures are reliable rather than inerrant. Thus the Bible may not always be literally accurate, but it can nevertheless be trusted. This view has been adopted because of a high level of confidence that the Hebrew Scriptures have been preserved with a reasonable degree of accuracy, or at least a level where it may be possible to glimpse the true meaning through careful study. Yes, some of the narratives may be etiological, allegorical or apocryphal, but there must have been some reason for their inclusion.

Some confidence in this approach can be gained from the words of an anonymous writer in *Bibliotheca Sacra* in the year 1914.[14] He or she examined the reliability of biblical evidence based on the principles of jurisprudence, the science that deals with the competency of what is proposed as evidence in a court of law. The writer concluded that the Bible can be legally regarded as a properly preserved ancient document, and therefore the eyewitness reports, being accurately recorded, are admissible as evidence.

12. *Christian Theology*, 200.

13. *Let the Reader Understand*, 30.

14. *Studies in Theology*, 105–31.

The need for careful exegesis when trying to interpret biblical texts has already been mentioned several times. This procedure involves several stages of analysis (or criticisms as they are generally referred to by scholars), such as those described by Erickson.[15] Researchers select those that are most pertinent to their needs. Examples are as follows:

HISTORICAL CRITICISM

Exploring the historical setting, customs, and culture pertaining at the time the text was written. Sometimes an earlier historical event prompted a later writer to comment on the repercussions or aftermath of this. If available, archeological or non-biblical sources can help to date an event.

LITERARY CRITICISM

Determining the genre in which the text falls, which can then help to determine its purpose. For the Scriptures, the genres include historical narratives, the law, wisdom, poetry, prophecy, and apocalyptic predictions (see also chapter 4). This sort of analysis may also help to identify the source or precursor of a text. Sometimes there are clues, for example a certain writer may use specific names for God, such as Yahweh or Elohim, and so texts by the same individual can be brought together. Additionally, study may indicate how the writer used words in order for them to have an emotive or moral effect on the reader.

FORM CRITICISM

This is mostly an extension of the previous two criticisms, including trying to identify any precursor, or oral tradition, on which the text could be based. Sometimes an editor could have tried to fit several vague stories together to create a coherent whole. Also,

15. *Christian Theology,* 84–102.

a later writer may have added explanations that were not included in the original version. In some instances the same text or narrative appears in different parts of the Bible, but in different forms. Identifying these can significantly help in the analysis.

TEXTURAL CRITICISM

In the effort to try and establish as far as possible what was first written, different manuscripts and translations need to be consulted. For example, the lack of complete agreement between the LXX and MT texts has already been mentioned, and even relatively modern translations differ. It is the task of the exegete to compare as many versions as possible to try and determine the most accurate rendition.

REDACTION CRITICISM

This is related to textural criticism, but it makes use of the parallel or similar versions of a narrative that appear in the Bible. In the New Testament, the four Gospel writers sometimes report the same story but from different angles, being influenced by their particular theological concern. This is only rarely the case with the Hebrew Scriptures, but the same topic is sometimes mentioned in more than one book, for example the Ten Commandments appear in both Exodus and Deuteronomy. Also, one writer may refer to the text of an earlier one, using slightly different language. Jesus often quoted the Scriptures, helping to clarify their meanings, and this can be helpful to the exegete.

In conclusion, can we ever be sure that our efforts have even brought us close to understanding what the original biblical writer wrote, at the time, for a particular audience and for a particular purpose? It is doubtful if we can completely achieve this goal, which is what makes the journey interesting and challenging to the scholar. We can, however, try and come ever closer to the truth. *The Hermeneutical Spiral* is a book by Grant R. Osborne (2016). His approach to exegesis is that it entails a spiral from text to context. He opines that interpretation is not a closed circle, but it is an open-ended movement that spirals nearer and nearer to the text's original meaning. This will be the present writer's aim, and it is hoped that the quest to be described in subsequent chapters will inform on the nature of God, and his origin.

Chapter 4 ∾

History of the Books Consulted

As MENTIONED IN CHAPTER 2, the first five books of the Scriptures are believed by many to have been written by Moses in about 1,440 BCE. Known as the Pentateuch, or Torah, they include descriptions of events that occurred some 500 years earlier that had been preserved by oral tradition.

However, some dispute this. Grant[1] reports that some nineteenth century scholars concluded that the early writings came not from Moses, but from four documentary sources. The first two were respectively named as J (Yawist), and E (Elohist), based on the preferred names for God being used by these writers. The third was P (Priestly Writer), and there was supplementary material from D, the author responsible not only for the book of Deuteronomy but probably also for deuteronomistic history that is contained in Joshua ranging through to Kings.[2]

The Yawist seems to be the main writer of the earliest narratives, but is believed to have lived as recently as the tenth century before Christ—about 400 years after Moses. He probably drew on some earlier written, as well as oral, sources, and started at the beginning with the story of Adam and Eve. The fact that he was writing about events that occurred some 1,000 years before his time,

1. *The History of Ancient Israel*, 96–9.
2. McCartney & Clayton, *Let the Reader Understand*, 307.

means there were plenty of opportunities for the stories to have been twisted, edited, corrupted, embellished, or even completely fabricated before being penned.

It has also been suggested that Ezra the priest, along with his assistant Nehemiah, was responsible for selecting and editing the Scriptures that were to be accepted into the Hebrew canon. Although many of the books already existed, Ezra may have added to the text, for example the concluding section of Deuteronomy that concerns the death of Moses.[3] Ezra also wrote the book named after him, and may have written the two Chronicles books.

The collection of Scriptures was subsequently extended by the addition of a few more books over the next 100 years. If, however, Ezra was responsible for compiling the bulk of the collection, then it would have taken place in the fifth century BCE. This would bring forward the date of the final editing of many of the accounts by about another 500 years. It is inevitable that the chances of errors and changes occurring in the descriptions of events that happened up to 1,500 years previously would have increased accordingly.

How confident can we be that the earliest five, or even 10, books of the Scriptures, preserved only by oral tradition before they were written down, were not simply myths and therefore should not be taken seriously? Perhaps it is unfair to imply this, as myths often have factual bases, and may be found on subsequent research to be surprisingly accurate. Even if the events had not actually occurred, there could still be meaningful messages disguised as allegory, apocrypha, or etiology, which would hold important meanings for the adherents of the Abrahamic faiths.

There are 24 books in the Hebrew Bible, but 39 in the Protestant Old Testament. Although the texts are essentially the same, they are categorized somewhat differently in the two collections. The books were only included in the canon if they were believed to have been written by prophets or visionaries who had either received the words, or at least inspiration, directly from God. The exegesis to be described in subsequent chapters will, therefore, be

3. Anonymous, *www.askelm.com/restoring/res006.htm*

based on the premise that they do reveal something about God himself.

Because the Old Testament compilation was mostly used for the present study (except when consulting the LXX translation), the citations will follow the conventions, and the order, adopted by that version of the scriptures. All but five of the 39 books yielded pertinent quotations, and Table 1 shows these listed under their respective genres. Note that two entries appear each for the books of Exodus, Jonah, and Daniel. The former can be split into two halves, with chapters 1 to 19 being historical narrative, and chapters 20–40 relating to the law. The contents of the other two books overlap different genres, as will be explained later in this chapter.

Table 1. Hebrew Scripture books used, and their genres

Historical	The Law	Wisdom	Poetry	Prophecy	Apocalyptic
Genesis	Exodus	Job	Psalms	Isaiah	Daniel
Exodus	Leviticus	Proverbs	Song of Sol	Jeremiah	
Numbers	Deuteronomy	Ecclesiastes	Lamentations	Ezekiel	
Joshua				Daniel	
Judges				Hosea	
1 Samuel				Joel	
2 Samuel				Amos	
1 Kings				Jonah	
2 Kings				Micah	
1 Chron				Habakkuk	
2 Chron				Zephaniah	
Nehemiah				Haggai	
Jonah				Zechariah	
				Malachi	

Before embarking on the analysis, and to help put them into perspective, a brief description will be given of the history, author, and content of each of the 34 books used. However, it is rare for scholars to agree on these details. Even when a prophet's name is included in the book itself, and historical events mentioned that can now be dated, it is possible that later writers or editors could have drawn on older fragments when compiling a more retrospective account. Whilst the order of the books was no doubt intended to reflect a chronological narrative, a more recent understanding of biblical history has sometimes disrupted what was probably once an accepted timeline.

GENESIS

This first book in the Pentateuch, traditionally ascribed to Moses, commences with the story of creation, the birth of Adam and Eve, and the events relating to Noah and the flood. From chapter 12 the narrative changes to recount the saga of Abraham. Some text must have been added more recently, for example chapter 36:31–43 that lists the whole geniality of the kings of Edom, stretching until after Moses would have died[4] . After Abraham died, the exploits of his son Isaac, grandson Jacob, and his children, including Joseph, are related. This includes the latter being sold into slavery in Egypt, only for the family to follow later in order to escape the severe famine in Canaan.

EXODUS

The Israelites fled Egypt to escape from harsh treatment and slavery, after God had inflicted 10 plagues on the Egyptians. However, they are followed by their captors, but the soldiers perish when crossing the Red Sea (or Reed Sea). Moses receives the 10 Commandments on Mount Sinai, and makes a covenant with God. The Israelites continue their journey for 40 years. Moses was not allowed by God to enter the Promised Land. Non-biblical Egyptian writings mention a nomadic people called Habiru entering Egypt to escape famine. According to Butler,[5] the exodus may have occurred during the reign of Rameses 11 (1304–1236 BCE), although some favor a date some 100 years earlier.

4. Wenham, *Genesis,* 55.
5. *Holman Concise Bible Dictionary,* 211.

LEVITICUS

The tribe of Levi, who was a son of Jacob, was given the responsibility for maintaining the priesthood, as a reward for supporting Moses. Instructions are provided on ordination of the priests, the various sacrificial procedures, and what is clean and unclean. Their purpose is to ensure that the covenant relationship between the Israelites and God was maintained. The book concludes with directives on how the people of the Holy God have to live as distinct from others in the land.

NUMBERS

The preparation needed to proceed to the Promised Land, the journey there, and the inheritance once they arrived, are described. Much of this involved numbering and organizing the people, the allotting of land to the different tribes, and what offerings to make when they had inherited it. Numbers serves the role of describing the transition from the old generation that left Egypt, to the new one poised to enter Canaan.[6]

DEUTERONOMY

Moses gives several speeches to his people, starting with a review of their journey thus far, and ending with a renewal of the covenant made with God. In the middle portion, 613 commandments are listed. These are mostly instructions to be used for life in Canaan, rather than laws to be used in legal cases.[7] Some of these concern capital punishment or cruel sacrifices. Ian Wilson argues that: "From heaven he made you hear his voice . . . on earth he showed you his great fire" (4:36), shows that the deuteronomists accepted that God can exist simultaneously in heaven and on earth.[8]

6. Longman & Dillard, *An Introduction to the Old Testament*, 92.
7. Butler, *Holman Concise Bible Dictionary*, 161.
8. *Divine Presence in Deuteronomy*, 403–7.

JOSHUA

This describes the Israelites' conquest of Canaan, the Promised Land, under their new leader Joshua. The suggested dates for this range from 1451 to 1260 BCE. As the book ends with a mention of Joshua's death, this must have been added later by another writer. Notable events include the fall of Jericho, and the renewal of the covenant at Shechem.

JUDGES

Tradition favors the author as the prophet Samuel, who is believed to have lived in the pre-monarchy period, near the beginning of the second millennium BCE. Some scholars believe it was written several hundred years later, by an author who could have drawn on earlier manuscripts. This book relates the early days of life in the Promised Land when military leaders, or judges, tried to keep order.

1 & 2 SAMUEL

Samuel lived about 1075–1000 BCE, and he may have written some of the text, but a multiple authorship over a long period has also been suggested.[9] Samuel's own death, mentioned in 1 Sam (25:1), must have been added by another writer. He received God's call at an early age, whilst being raised by Eli (1 Sam, 3:4–15), and became the last of the judges before the Israelites demanded a king to lead them. Samuel firstly anointed Saul, and then David who, despite many faults, gained favor with God and was a popular leader.

9. Butler, *Holman Concise Bible Dictionary*, 533.

1 & 2 KINGS

Bimson (2011, p. 334) notes that the final version of the two books cannot have been written before 561 BCE, because the release of King Jehoiachin from prison in that year is recorded (2 Kgs 25:27). One suggested author is the prophet Jeremiah (although he died about 570 BCE). Between them, the books detail a succession of kings of Israel (in the north) and Judah (in the south), starting with David (reigned 1010–970 BCE), who was king of the combined nation. In 930 BCE the country then divided. Hoshea was the last king of Israel (732–722 BCE), and Zedekiah, the final ruler of Judah (597–586 BCE). Each king is judged according to his faithfulness to God, and the underlying message is one of hope and consolation, despite the nations being conquered.

1 & 2 CHRONICLES

These may have been written by the prophet Ezra, which would place them around 538–520 BCE, although some favor a later date. As the name suggest, the books chronicle the events of history up to that time, starting with Adam, but from a different perspective from what has been covered in Samuel and Kings. Book 1 continues with the story of David, and lists the genealogy of Solomon and some of the other kings. Preparations for building the Jerusalem temple, and the organization of the priests and Levites, are described. Book 2 includes and division of the nation after Solomon's death, and ends with the fall of Jerusalem in 586 BCE.

NEHEMIAH

This could have been written by Nehemiah, or Ezra, or both, at a date some time between about 458 and 398 BCE. It recounts the rebuilding of the walls of Jerusalem under Nehemiah's leadership. The prophet relies on God to guide him, and frequently prays to him.

JOB

There are no clues to indicate the author or date of this book, although David Clines[10] suggests the outer limits of its date are the seventh and second centuries BCE. He opines that the story may have been based on an earlier folk tale, and that the central character appears to be from the patriarchal biblical period, before the time of Moses. The theme is one of the suffering of innocent people, and it may symbolise the experiences of the Jews in the time of exile. But this will not last for ever; God does still care for us, and we should not abandon him.

PSALMS

The 150 Psalms were probably written by several authors over a period ranging from about 1060 to 444 BCE. Although many are attributed to King David, and some to Moses, Solomon and others, some doubt that those named were the actual authors.[11] The Psalms are divided into five groups including hymns of praise and worship, thanksgiving, prayers for help and salvation, and pleas for forgiveness. Michael Barber and colleagues[12] suggest that the Last Supper was a Passover meal, and that Jesus and his disciples would have sung the Hallel Psalms (113–118).

PROVERBS

The text states that Solomon (c 971–931 BCE) was the author, although Butler[13] opines that at least some parts were written over a period of several hundred years, perhaps from before Solomon to 700 BCE or later. The presence of different genres supports this notion, as the book contains long wisdom poems, brief sayings,

---

10. *Job*, 460.

11. Longman & Dillard, *An Introduction to the Old Testament*, 242.

12. *What Did Jesus Sing at the Last Supper?*

13. *Holman Concise Bible Dictionary*, 512.

and admonitions. These provide some insight into the Israelites' view of a wise person, and they generally operate on the principle that you reap the consequences of what you do.

ECCLESIASTES

The opening verse gives a strong hint that Solomon was the author in circa 965 BCE, but some think this book was compiled or edited much more recently. The content is often pessimistic, but may nevertheless provide solace to those who wonder why God allows injustices to happen.

SONG OF SOLOMON

Some sources prefer *Song of Songs* as the title of this collection of love poems, and attribute the authorship to Hezekiah (787–716 BCE) rather than Solomon himself. Although they are displayed as being sung by a man to a woman, and vice versa, there is a view that they represent the relationship between God and his people of Israel.[14]

ISAIAH

The prophet was probably born in Jerusalem in about 760 BCE, and is generally accepted as the initial author, but other writers may also have been involved. Despite Isaiah's attempted intervention, Israel was destroyed by the Assyrians in 722 BCE. He warns of a similar fate for Judah, and anticipates the exile into Babylon (586 BCE). The mention of King Cyrus (45:1), who was to allow the captives to return in 539 BCE, suggests this was a later addition, as it was long after Isaiah's death in about 700 BCE.[15] The overall themes covered in the book are social justice, trust in God, and salvation.

14. Ibid., 577.
15. Kidner, *Isaiah*, 629–32.

JEREMIAH

He was born at Anathoth, near Jerusalem, around 640 BCE or later. Although the text contains biographical detail, Arnold[16] reviews suggestions of a multiple authorship. The book states that some of Jeremiah's words were dictated to the scribe Baruch (45:1), who may have subsequently added to, or edited, the text. The prophet warns that Judah will fall unless the people abandon idolatry and remain faithful to God. However, the country is conquered by the Babylonians, the temple destroyed, and the people exiled. Jeremiah still preached a message of hope that Israel will eventually be restored, and that God will write a new covenant.

LAMENTATIONS

Traditionally, Jeremiah is accepted as the author, perhaps around 584 BCE. Jerusalem had been destroyed two years earlier, and the book laments this. But it also maintains a trust on God and hope for the future.

EZEKIEL

He was born in Judah prior to the conquest, and warned the people of the impending judgment, due to their apostasy. Ezekiel was taken captive to Babylon in 597 BCE, but preached messages of encouragement and hope for the future. The book includes descriptions of visions, symbolism, allegory, and apocalyptic predictions, as well as accounts of his own strange behavior.[17]

DANIEL

Traditionally Daniel is acknowledged as the author, some time between 605 and 468 BCE. The first part is prophecy, and

16. *Recent trends in the study of Jeremiah*, 76–83.
17. Butler, *Holman Concise Bible Dictionary*, 214–5.

encouragement during the Judean exile to retain confidence that God will set them free. The second part is apocalyptic, and contains descriptions of surrealistic visions of the "end time" and the ultimate victory of God's people.

HOSEA

This is the first of the 10 Minor Prophets consulted for this enquiry. Hosea (circa 755–722 BCE) was one of several Northern Kingdom prophets who warned against the consequences of being unfaithful to the Lord. The message is that God will punish the people for their sins, but he will later restore their relationship with him.

JOEL

The author is assumed to be the Judean prophet of the same name, with suggested dates of composition ranging from 800 to 400 BCE. These embrace both the destruction of the Jerusalem temple in 586 BCE, and its rebuilding some 70 years later. A terrible locust plague is described (1:1—2:17), which Joel interpreted as a warning from God that the people must return to him. The Lord then said he would show pity on those who repented, and removes the plague.[18]

AMOS

Verse 1 identifies Amos as the author, and that he was born in Tekoa, probably in Judah. He is believed to have been active around 760–753 BCE, although some favor a later date. His mission was to travel to Israel to warn the people of a catastrophe unless they refrained from apostasy. As he probably died in 745 BCE, he did not live to witness the Assyrian invasion in 722 BCE, but his book ends with a message of hope and restoration. Hiebert[19] (1996) speculates that these words could have been added later.

18. Ibid, 361.
19. *Amos,* In Elwell (Ed.)

JONAH

This book is both narrative and prophesy. It may have been written by Jonah himself in about 785–753 BCE. It tells of the prophet's reticence in obeying God's instruction to go to Nineveh, but also of God's sovereignty, love, and mercy. Alternatively, it may be post-Exilic, and relate to the Jews being swallowed into the Babylonian empire, but then being given a second chance (Jewell, 2017, pers com).

MICAH

The author is identified in the text, but there may be later additions. His ministry can be computed from the kings mentioned there, and they range from about 740 to 687 BCE. Micah warned Judah that it could face the same fate as did Israel for its apostasy and exploitation of the poor, although he still believed there was hope for the future. Micah prophesized the coming of a new ruler, which Matthew saw as a description of Christ (Matt 2:6).[20]

HABAKKUK

The author of the same name is stated in verse 1 of the book. If the message was contemporary with the events described, it would date from about 600 BCE.[21] Habakkuk questioned God on why he does not punish the Babylonians for being so cruel. The response is that he will take action in his own good time, and he commends those who remain faithful to him.

ZEPHANIAH

This prophet ministered around 640–609 BCE. As did several other prophets, he warns of Judah's (and other nations') destruction

20. Butler, *Holman Concise Bible Dictionary*, 424–5.
21. Baker, *Habakkuk*, 840.

for worshiping false gods, but also that Jerusalem will eventually be restored.

HAGGAI

Haggai's ministry dates from about 520 BCE, by which time the Judean exiles had been allowed to return. However, apathy had delayed the rebuilding of the Jerusalem temple. He urges the people to do so, and to stop neglecting God whilst pursuing selfish concerns. He assures them of God's presence and approval.[22]

ZECHARIAH

He was a contemporary of Haggai (circa 520 BCE). God had instructed both of them to press for completion of the temple restoration. John James[23] states that Zechariah had a two-fold message: remember the past when their ancestors sinned, and return to the Lord. The book contains several visions that depict a prosperous future, provided the Judeans learn from their mistakes and purify themselves from sin.[24]

MALACHI

This final book is also the youngest, dating from about 450 BCE. Although Nehemiah is not specifically mentioned, the sins cited in his book may have inspired the messages of Malachi. These include a corrupt priesthood, inter-marriage, and failure to pay tithes. Malachi assures the people that God still loves them, but warned that judgment would come unless they repented.[25]

---

22. James, *Haggai, Zechariah and Malachi*, 28–36.

23. Ibid, 50–1.

24. Butler, *Holman Concise Bible Dictionary*, 648–9.

25. James, *Haggai, Zechariah and Malachi*, 142–3.

Chapter 5 ❧

God's Origin, and Name

THE QUEST TO LEARN something about the nature of God, in the way that it is being attempted here, may bring a wry smile to the faces of those who are Christians and acknowledge Jesus Christ as the son of God. As mentioned earlier, such believers would surely say that all you have to do is study what Jesus said and did, as recorded in the New Testament, and you will have all the answers you need. But, it as was pointed out, those such as the Jews and Muslims, who acknowledge the God of Abraham but regard Jesus as only another prophet, would not be convinced by the outcome of this relatively simple approach.

Because this book is intended to serve adherents of each of the Abrahamic religions, plus any others who may be interested, the exegesis will concentrate on the sources in the Hebrew Scriptures (Old Testament). The New Testament will be consulted occasionally, such as when it provides some clarification for what is written in its older companion, but it will not be used as the primary source. However, the opportunity will remain for Christians to add to, or reinforce, the findings by consulting New Testament, if they so wish.

Before proceeding with the attempt to identify some attributes of the Abrahamic God, it might be helpful to recall what was discussed in the earlier chapters about his origin. The idea of a supreme being might have first arisen from the notion of a force that controls nature. The annual cycle of crop growing and animal breeding was vital to the survival of early humans, and it still is. Veneration of objects such as the sun or moon might have been regarded as necessary to help ensure a regular supply of food.

Another early influence could have been the need to try and account for the inexplicable, in order to avoid that uncomfortable feeling of cognitive dissonance. A belief in the existence of an all-controlling, powerful entity would have eliminated the need to try and find a logical explanation for events. It is reasonable to assume that, if a god of some kind had been conceived, then it would seem advisable to perform rituals to keep this being happy, and to worship idols or images that represent it.

It was suggested that the idea of a soul that survives death might have arisen in order to try and account for phenomena such as dreams or breathing. Once this had been acknowledged, then it would have been a logical next step to have burial practices that afforded the soul an opportunity to leave the body and continue safely on its journey. As discussed in chapter 1, evidence that this was the case stems from the excavation of burial sites that date back 100,000 years. Also, figurines, that are believed to be 30,000 old, have been discovered that may have been the objects of idol worship.

The question of the origins of the Abrahamic God—the God of the Scriptures—is influenced by a number of key considerations. It depends first of all on whether or not we believe the one described is *the* authentic, Supreme Being. If not, then is this just a hypothetical creation that can be used to account for things that modern science and technology cannot explain? After all, this is how the ancients may have conceived the idea of a god, and thus avoided that uncomfortable cognitive dissonance.

Another idea, for those who prefer a secular explanation, is that God was an inhabitant from another world, who once visited the earth. The book by Eric Von Däniken *Chariots of the Gods: Was God an Astronaut?* (New York: Berkley Books, 1968) intrigued many readers with its description of archaeological artifacts, carvings, and geographical features on earth that seemed to point to alien visitations.

Some early cave art depicts strange-looking humanoid figures, and the present author obtained an Aboriginal sketch during a visit to Australia. It is crudely painted in dark brown, on a piece of pink slate measuring approximately 15 by 12 centimeters (see Figure 2). Although no details were available concerning what the artist intended to depict, it is possible it could be a representation of a mythical being that, according to legend, once interacted with the local inhabitants.

Similar images were created by the San (Bushmen) people of southern Africa, who started making rock paintings about 30,000 years ago. A photograph taken by the author of one of many examples is shown in Figure 3. The date it was created is not known, but it seems to depict both human and animal features. Is there some spiritual significance in this? Could it represent an alien being?

Figure 2. Aboriginal Depiction of a Humanoid Figure
(Author's image)

Figure 3. Rock painting by San Bushmen
(Author's image)

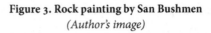

Figure 3. Rock painting by San Bushmen
(Author's image)

Although the idea of visitations from other inhabited worlds may seem fanciful, if not completely ridiculous, those who subscribe to this idea can cite Bible references to support their belief. For example, Exodus 13:21 states, "By day the Lord went ahead of them in a pillar of cloud to guide them on their way and by night in a pillar of fire." This image continues in the following chapter, verse 24: "The Lord looked down from the pillar of fire and cloud at the Egyptian army."

An even more pertinent text appears in chapter 19, verse18 of the same book, which could easily be a description of a modern space rocket landing. It states, "Mount Sinai was covered in smoke, because the Lord descended on it in fire. The smoke billowed up . . . like smoke from a furnace, and the whole mountain trembled violently." Finally, 2 Kings 2:22 relates what could be a rather naïve description of a rocket launch: "Suddenly a chariot of fire and horses of fire appeared and separated the two of them, (Elisha and Elijah) and Elijah went up to heaven in a whirlwind."

For those who do accept that God is the unique deity portrayed as such in the Bible, the question is: what was the origin of this Supreme Being? It was also mentioned earlier that, although this entity is generally referred to in the Scriptures by the masculine *he*, and Jesus often mentioned *The Father*, these epithets are no doubt the product of the patriarchal society pertaining at the time the texts were written. It is doubtful that gender can be applied to the biblical God but, purely for the sake of convenience, the present account will maintain the common practice of referring to the godhead using the masculine pronoun.

To return to the question, we simply do not know if he communicated with our ancestors from 100,000 or so years ago, and influenced their burial practices. The earliest written account we have of God's intervention with human beings is that in the Pentateuch which, as discussed earlier, may have been written by Moses in the fifteenth century BCE, or more recently. These books describe events that were purported to have occurred earlier, the records of which were preserved through oral tradition. If the accounts are literally true, then the first recorded words of God would have been those spoken to Adam and his family. Several generations later we have the story of Noah, and God's conversations with him. However, some believe these stories should not be taken as facts, but rather be regarded as apocryphal.

We may be on firmer ground with the story of Abraham's call, as this forms part of the origins and history of the Jewish nation that runs like a thread through the whole of the Hebrew Scriptures. If Abraham was indeed the first person to receive a message direct from God, then this would place the beginning of the communication between the deity and humans as being somewhere around 2,000 BCE, or maybe a little later.

Have we come any closer to determining the time when God first appeared? Perhaps, for many readers, we have not, despite the range of dates offered in the foregoing discussion. It might be that we just have to be content with the statements in the opening verses of Genesis and, more succinctly, the Gospel of John: "In the beginning was the Word, and the Word was with God, and the Word was God" (1:1). The more liberal translation of the *Good News Bible* (GNB) reads: "Before the world was created, the Word already existed; he was with God, and he was the same as God." Psalm 90:2 has a similar message: "Before the mountains were born, or you brought forth the whole world, from everlasting to everlasting you are God."

The only difficulty with this answer is whether or not the mind can accept that there was something that had no beginning, but had always existed. We feel very uncomfortable when there is no neat answer to questions of this nature. Perhaps it is best to just accept it on trust, and acknowledge that it is beyond the capability of the human mind to understand how anything could have had no beginning. It gives one a new respect for the writer of John's Gospel, for the way he simply explained how it all began.

ॐ

Having perhaps gone as far as we can exploring the origin of gods in general, and the Abrahamic God in particular, we need to pause and ask: what is the name of this deity whom we have been discussing? *God*, even spelled with a capital letter, is a general term and not a specific name. Jesus is a specific name, but what is his heavenly father called?

The Lord is a term used frequently in the Bible, including by God himself. A particularly relevant quotation occurs in Exodus, 3:13–15. Moses asked God what answer he should give to the Israelites if they ask what he is called. God replied, "I am who I am (or, "I am the One who is")." He then added, "Say to the Israelites, 'The Lord, the God of your fathers . . . has sent me to you . . . This is my name for ever, the name you shall call me.'" A similar quotation occurs in Isaiah 42:8, "I am the Lord, that is my name." Does this answer the question? Not really, because the names Lord and God may each be specific when they are linked to a person's name but, on their own, they are just titles that can be applied to any number of people.

When discussing the reliability of the Hebrew Scriptures in chapter 3, it was mentioned that some biblical writers use the term Yahweh for God, and others Elohim. The former name appeared in the original Hebrew versions, and is spelled YHWH as the vowels were omitted from that early written language. In English Bibles it is usually translated as Lord, although sometimes Jehovah in the King James Version, for example: "But my name Jehovah was not known to them." (Ex 6:3). Likewise, Elohim is a Hebrew word suggesting majesty, and a God of many parts[1] but, again, in most modern versions, it is rendered as Lord.

An exception is the *Aramaic Bible in Plain English*. In this translation, the Hebrew names are sometimes retained. For example, "So Yahweh has fulfilled what he promised," whereas the NIV has "The Lord has kept the promise he made" (2 Chron, 6:10). One of the passages where the other name appears is Jonah (4:6), "And Jehovah Elohim prepared a gourd" ("Then the Lord God provided a leafy plant"—NIV). In all the instances where Elohim appears in the Aramaic version, it is preceded by Jehovah, as in the above example.

A personal discussion with Rabbi Tully Bryks (5th October, 2016), founder and director of *Rabbi With Answers*, revealed the Jewish standpoint on God's names. He said that there are many such names, and these are inter-dispersed throughout the Torah (Pentateuch). This suggests these five books were written by the same author—traditionally believed to be Moses—being dictated word for word from God. The names include Hashem (representing mercy), Ado-nai (the master of all, or royalty), and Elokim (or Elohim) representing judgment and nature. Rabbi Bryks noted that the latter name conveys the notion that all individual things in the world, although they may seem unconnected, are really all unified through God.

An Islamic source concurs with the view that neither Yahweh, Elohim, Jehovah, nor Lord are the original names of God

---

1. Erickson, *Christian Theology*, 328–9

Almighty, but are simply courtesy titles for him, or descriptions of his qualities.[2] Interestingly, however, it states that there is a name for God: it is Allah. To support this claim, the anonymous author firstly explains that God in Arabic and Aramaic sound the same, and it is Allah. Secondly, he or she notes that, when Jesus cried out from the cross, he addressed God as Eloi, which is derived from Elaw or Allah. The NIV Bible actually renders Matthew 27:46 thus: "Jesus cried out in a loud voice, *Eli, Eli, lema sabachthani?* (which means 'My God, My God, why have you forsaken me?')," although it notes that some Greek manuscripts have Eloi instead of Eli).

Whilst this discovery, that God's actual name is Allah could be a profound revelation, its impact is somewhat dampened when the Islamic writer states that this name means *The Supreme God Almighty* in Arabic. This is in keeping with the English interpretation added in parentheses after the vernacular cry of Jesus. One can thus be forgiven for thinking that maybe the quest to discover God's real name is not yet over.

Although Exodus (6:3) states that God said to Moses, "But by my name the Lord," the NIV adds a footnote stating that the original Hebrew used the name *El-Shaddai*. It may be unfortunate that alternative names such as this are not generally preserved in English translations, as there could be some significance in their use. The meaning of *El-Shaddai* is not certain, and it may stimulate an avenue of research.

Another interesting example of a different name occurs in Exodus (34:14), namely: "The Lord, whose name is Jealous, is a jealous God." Now, why should the same word be used as a proper name, and an adjective, especially in the same sentence? The LXX text is slightly different: "The Lord God, a jealous name, is a jealous God." The Greek *zeltes* is best translated as zealous, or eager, and usually refers to being stirred into action by emotion.[3] Thus, Jealous is not so much a proper name, but rather it implies a God who is protective, and keen to discourage the worship of false gods. As

2. Anonymous, *Islam: the true religion*

3. Friberg, Friberg & Miller, *Analytical Lexicon of the Greek New Testament*, 185.

Butler states, he takes himself seriously, and wants others to also take him seriously.[4]

Perhaps the final contribution on the quest to discover God's name should be drawn from the article, "The meaning of the 'name' of God," by Christopher Howse.[5] Howse's thesis is that God's name signifies his presence, not his actual moniker. There are several Bible passages that support this view, starting with the Lord's Prayer: "Hallowed be thy name" (Matthew, 6:9–13). God's reply to Moses when he asked for his name: "I am who I am" (Exodus 3:13–15) has already been mentioned. Then in Deuteronomy (12:11) God says that he will choose a dwelling place for his name. In St John's Gospel, the King James Version, it states, "I have declared unto them thy name, and will declare it" (17:26), and the translation from the Greek Septuagint is, "I made your name known to them, and I will make it known." However, the NIV omits "name" and renders the verse "I have made you known to them, and will continue to make you known."

The conclusion that Howse draws from this is that, when the texts use the words "name of God," they indicate an immanence, or presence among human kind. The above quote from Deuteronomy specifically mentions a dwelling place for his name: if that was where his name would be, then that will also be the place of his presence. It may be significant that we use the word "name" quite often in our devotions. The Lord's Prayer was mentioned above, and we baptize infants "in the name of the Father, Son and Holy Ghost."

It may thus be futile to continue to ponder the real name of God, assuming he has one, and be content to continue to use names that are either courtesy titles, or that reflect one or more of the divine qualities. And when we know of a place where God's name dwells, we can rejoice that his presence will be there also.

---

4. *Holman Concise Bible Dictionary*, 269.

5. UK *Daily Telegraph*, 37.

Chapter 6 ◆

God's Attributes

THIS CHAPTER IS CONCERNED with what God *is*, rather than what he *does*—these activities will be discussed in later chapters. Among the qualities frequently applied to him are: *omnipotent* (all powerful), *omniscient* (all knowing), and *omnipresent* (present always and everywhere). Interestingly, these specific words are absent from most modern English translations of the Bible, and only omnipotent appears (once) in the King James' Version (Rev 19:6). Here, the Greek word used, *pantokratōr*, can also be translated as the almighty, or the all-powerful one. This implies that there is only a single being that can be described in this way.

The characteristics we are concerned with here are defined by Erickson as "permanent qualities . . . the very essence of God." [1] Some may say that the main attributes of God are so well known, they do not need a whole chapter in which to unpack them. After all, we only have to look at the life of Jesus, his son, to learn about his father. Nevertheless, it will help our total understanding if we do make the effort to remind ourselves of how God is referred to in the older Scriptures—the text that is accepted by Christians, Jews, and Muslims alike. To help clarify just what the original writers intended, where necessary the Greek words used in the LXX version will be consulted, as well as the English translations based on the MT.

1. *Christian Theology*, 265.

Butler[2] lists examples of terms that can be used to describe God. First and foremost, he is *unique*, the only one, and he has always been there. Isaiah makes this clear: "This is what the Lord says . . . 'I am the first and the last; apart from me there is no God'" (44:6). This is reiterated in 45:18, "I am the Lord, and there is no other," and in 48:12, "I am he; I am the first and I am the last." A statement by Jeremiah also implies that the God we know is unique: "But the Lord is the true God" (10:10). Psalm 90, a designated prayer of Moses, states, "Before the mountains were born, or you brought forth the whole world, from everlasting to everlasting you are God" (verse 2), and "A thousand years in your sight are like a day that has just gone by" (verse 4).

No doubt the most oft' quoted references to God's longevity have already been mentioned, in relation to his origin. It is stated at the start of Genesis, and confirmed in the Gospel of John, that he was there right from the start of things. Psalm 102 is specific about God's *endurance*, with the statement, "They will perish, but you will remain . . . you remain the same, and your years will never end" (verses 26–27).

There are several references to God being *holy*, for example, "I am the Lord your God . . . I am holy" (Lev 11:44). In 1 Sam (2:2) we read, "There is no one holy like the Lord," and in Isaiah (6:3), "Holy, holy, holy is the Lord Almighty." But what does it mean to be holy? It is a unique characteristic that belongs only to God, and implies being completely divorced from everything sinful and evil, and being always perfect and doing what is right. The Greek for holy, *agios*, also means dedicated and sacred. The total perfection implied by this is only achievable by God, although we humans can strive to follow his example as far as we are able.

Not only is God holy, but he is *majestic*, so states the author of Exodus (15:11), "(you are) majestic in holiness, awesome in glory." The Greek word *doxa*, used in the LXX version, also means radiance, splendor, and glory, and this characteristic epithet is repeated elsewhere in Scriptures. When the people had heard the

2. *Holman Concise Bible Dictionary*, 268–9.

Ten Commandments they said to Moses, "The Lord our God has shown us his glory and majesty" (Deut 5:24).

As might be expected, several Psalms sing praises to God's majesty. For example, "Lord, our Lord, how majestic is your name in all the earth" (8:1), which is repeated in verse 9. Psalm 29:4 states, "The voice of the Lord is powerful, the voice of the Lord is majestic." The Songs of Songs (or Song of Solomon) is written as a poem of love between a man and a woman, although as stated earlier it could be a dialogue between God and the people of Israel. Verse 6:4 reads, "You are . . . as majestic as troupe with banners," and in verse 10, "Who is this that appears . . . (as) majestic as the stars in procession?"

The mention of *righteousness* in the above quotation from Proverbs, reminds us that this is another of God's attributes. The Greek word used for this, *dikaiosynē*, can also mean uprightness and just. Among the many textural references are: "(God says) my righteousness draws near speedily" (Isa 51:5); "You are always righteous, Lord (Jer 12:1); "I will see his righteousness" (Micah 7:9). The Psalms alone contain over 50 examples of this word, but what does it mean? Erickson[3] explains that it literally indicates "conforming to a given norm," and "living up to the standards of a relationship, especially with God." In other words, always doing what is right. It is often linked to the responsibility of fulfilling the obligations of a covenant, which God always did but the Israelites sometimes did not.

Thus, unlike holiness being the exclusive prerogative of the deity, human beings can also aspire to being righteous. Nevertheless, Jeremiah (11:20) makes it clear who is the role model: "But you, Lord Almighty, who judge righteously. . . . " This is echoed in Psalm 9, attributed to David; verse 4 reads, "For you have upheld my right and my cause, sitting enthroned as the righteous judge."

An adjective often synonymous with God is *sovereign*, usually coupled with Lord in modern English translations based on the MT. The term used in the Greek LXX version, *kyrios*, means Lord, Master, or God. The word sovereign denotes a ruler who is supreme, absolute, and total. Abraham refers to this when he made a request

3. *Christian Theology*, 955–6.

to his "Sovereign Lord" (Gen 15:2), and God referred to himself in this way when he instructed Moses to tell the people, "Three times a year all men are to appear before the Sovereign Lord" (Ex 23:17). Samuel reports that David prayed, "Who am I, Sovereign Lord" (2 Sam 7:18), and Isaiah the prophet proclaims, "See, the Sovereign Lord comes with power" (Isa 40:10). Jeremiah also uses this epithet in conjunction with power in the same breath when he prays, "Ah, Sovereign Lord, you have made the heavens and earth by your great power and outstretched arm" (Jer 32:17). Finally, Daniel (4:25) warns the people of the consequences of not acknowledging, "That the Most High is sovereign over all the kingdoms on earth."

A few more of the many other attributes of God can be mentioned, with a reminder that we are discussing what he *is*, or *has*, at this stage, not what he *does*. He has *grace*, which Butler defines as: "undeserved acceptance and love received from another, especially the characteristic attitude of God in providing salvation for sinners."[4] To this can be added guidance and help in times of need. This specific word does not appear in the Greek LXX version, and the meanings of those used in its place are slightly different. These include: *oiktirmōn* (compassionate and merciful), *egeēmōn* (merciful, compassionate, sympathetic), and *makrothymia* (patient, long-suffering).

The NIV Bible reports God as saying, "The Lord, the Lord, the compassionate and gracious God" (Ex 34:6). An episode of the ongoing story of Israel's trials and tribulations is reported in 2 Kings (13:23). Even though the country was being oppressed, "the Lord was gracious to them and had compassion." When the prophet Ezra entered Jerusalem, "The gracious hand of God was on him" (7:9). Nehemiah talks to God about the sinfulness of the Israelites, and says, "But you are a forgiving God, gracious and compassionate" (9:17). Once again, this attribute is mentioned in the Psalms, which, like several other quotations, links two terms. For example, "The Lord is compassionate and gracious" (103:8) and, "The Lord is gracious and compassionate" (145:8).

---

4. *Holman Concise Bible Dictionary*, 276.

A characteristic linked to grace and compassion is *love* which, including its derivatives, is mentioned in the Scriptures over 600 times. To name just a few, in Numbers (14:18) we read, "The Lord is slow to anger, abounding in love," and Deuteronomy mentions God keeping his covenant of love to a thousand generations of those who love him (7:9). This is a significant statement, as it is important that it is a reciprocal act. The name for love of this type is *agape*, which is in fact the Greek word used in the LXX. This distinguishes it from *philia*—brotherly (non-romantic) love, and *eros*—romantic affection. Psalms has many references, typical of which is, "The Lord is ... abounding in love" (103:8), and "His love endures for ever" (136:26).

Following on, in Proverbs (15:9) we read, "The Lord detests the way of the wicked, but he loves those who pursue righteousness." Isaiah (43:4) states that God says to Jacob and the people of Israel, "Since you are precious and honoured in my sight, and because I love you. . . . " Even the writer of the rather mournful Lamentations is able to write, "Because of the Lord's great love, we are not consumed" (3:22), and the minor prophet Zephaniah confirms that "The Lord your God is with you ... in his love he will no longer rebuke you" (3:17).

The list of the qualities or virtues that God has could no doubt include every positive adjective in the dictionary. However, before moving on to what the Lord *does*, just a few more examples of what he *is* will be mentioned here, to add to the growing number already discussed.

No compilation of God's attributes would be complete without *wisdom* (Greek *sophos* = wise), and this is mentioned by Job several times. In verse 9:4 we read, "His wisdom is profound, his power is vast" and, in 12:13, "To God belong wisdom and power." It is significant that, in both these verses, like some previous examples two virtues are linked. Job is intimating that it is necessary to have the ability to act on what the intellect decides, hence the omnipotence commonly ascribed to God. A little later on in his book, there is a whole chapter on the source of wisdom. Job asks the rhetorical question, "Where then does wisdom come from? Where does understanding dwell?" (28:20). He answers this himself three verses later, "God understands the way to it and he alone knows where it dwells."

Proverbs is liberally sprinkled with references to wisdom, including, "For the Lord gives wisdom; from his mouth comes knowledge and understanding" (2:6). The writer clearly understands the need to embrace this virtue when he exhorts his sons to, "Get wisdom, get understanding" (4:5). Isaiah obviously agrees, as he states, "All this comes from the Lord Almighty . . . whose wisdom is magnificent" (28:29).

Job also linked wisdom to power, and revisits this in 36:22 when he states, "God is exalted in his *power*," which he repeats in 37:23, "The Almighty is beyond our reach and exalted in power." Earlier in the Bible, God is reported to have said, "But I have raised you up . . . that I might show you my power" (Ex 9:16). Isaiah (40:10) states, "See, the Sovereign Lord comes with power," and Daniel (2:20), "Praise be to the name of God for ever and ever; wisdom and power are his." This is also a virtue that is acknowledged in several Psalms, including 61:11, "Power belongs to you, God," and 77:14, "You display your power among the peoples." *Kratos*, in the LXX version, can be translated as power, might, and dominion.

The Lord said to Moses, "I will have mercy on whom I will have mercy" (Ex 33:19). Thus, whilst God is merciful, his patience had been sorely tried by the sinfulness of some of the Israelites; it was his prerogative to show mercy only where he deemed it appropriate. Moses reminds the people of this, saying, "The Lord your God is a merciful God," adding: "He will not abandon or destroy you or forget the covenant" (Deut 4:31).

This concept of *mercy* is one repeated often in the Bible, especially with regard to Israelites. Psalm 78:38 again refers to their apostasy, stating: "Yet he was merciful; he forgave their iniquities." Likewise Daniel (9:9) writes, "The Lord our God is merciful and forgiving, even though we have rebelled against him."

In another context David, when he was distressed, has faith that God will look kindly on him: "Let me fall into the hands of the Lord, for his mercy is very great." (2 Sam, 24:14). Finally, when

Jerusalem had been devastated, Zechariah asks God how long he will withhold his mercy (1:12), to which the Lord replies, "I will return to Jerusalem with mercy, and there my house will be rebuilt" (1:16). In the Greek LXX version, mercy has a similar meaning to grace (vide supra). *Oiktiro* can be translated as having sympathy, compassion, and pity.

Although, with the attribute of mercy, we end this far-from-exhaustive trawl through the Scriptures to find qualities that can be applied to what God is, or has, we shall take a brief look at a slightly different approach to this survey. Rather than list adjectives that describe God, as has been done in this chapter, Erickson[5] classifies them under Attributes of Greatness. The first is *spirituality*, which is the quality of not being constrained by a physical body. Next there is *personality*, meaning that God is an individual being, with self-consciousness and will, capable of feeling, choosing, and entering into relationships with social beings like us. Erickson notes that such a quality is lacking in many Eastern religions.

Then there is *life*—God is alive, although he does not depend on anything outside of himself to sustain him. Several biblical reference attest to this attribute, including "I am who I am" (Ex 3:14), and "He is the living God" (Jer 10:10). Linked to this is that he is *eternal*. He is also *infinite*, he cannot be localized in time or space, and he can be anywhere and everywhere. Finally, he is *constant*, unchanging, as confirmed by several passage of scripture. For example, "You, Lord, sit enthroned for ever; your renown endures through all generations" (Psalm 101:12), and "I the Lord do not change" (Malachi 3:6).

As a reminder of 20 attributes that have been discussed in this chapter, according to the Hebrew Scriptures, God is:

> Omnipotent; omniscient; omnipresent; perfect; unique; enduring; holy; majestic; righteous; sovereign; gracious; loving; wise; merciful; spiritual; personable; living; eternal; infinite; constant.

It is now time to consider just what it is that God *does*.

5. *Christian Theology*, 266–81.

Chapter 7 ∾

What God Does—Creation

As HAS BEEN MENTIONED several times already, the book of Genesis commences with the statement that God was there "in the beginning," and then continues with a list of everything that he created. This account starts with what we can assume is the universe ("the heavens"), followed by the earth, and then all plants, animals, and finally human beings. There are over 100 references to creation in the Scriptures alone, some of which will be discussed in this chapter.

Although Evolutionists will have a different version of how flora and fauna developed, the really big issue concerns the beginning. Rabbi Tully Bryks (personal communication, 11th September, 2016) opines that you cannot properly ask such a question, because God created time. Thus, terms like before and after did not exist before the act of creation.

Religion and science are not too far apart on certain fundamental aspects of how it all started. The cosmologists' Big Bang theory on the origin of the universe does not necessarily disagree with the beliefs of the Creationists. In particular, the order that various aspects of the land, and then living plants and animals came along, share some common ground. The scientific view likewise acknowledges that that space and time only began when the bang occurred.

The difficulty of the human mind to grasp the meaning of terms such as infinity and timeless has already been touched upon in relation to God's origin. When we come to consider the commencement of everything, we again encounter the challenge of trying to comprehend what sparked the process off. If there was just an empty void, then we struggle to understand how something could have been created out of nothing. Logic tells us that, if there really was a time when there was absolutely nothing, then there would still be nothing now. Notwithstanding the impossibility of finding a satisfactory answer to questions such as these, we must nevertheless grasp the nettle and attempt to find some way of avoiding cognitive dissonance.

Many hours of contemplation and study have so far not improved on the opening verses of the book of Genesis, and John's Gospel. If we cannot conceive of there ever having been a time when absolutely nothing existed, then we have to accept that God was always there in the form of an invisible spirit. The secular equivalent would be that there was just energy without form. According to Albert Einstein's famous theory, energy can be transformed into matter, and matter can be transformed into energy $(E=MC^2)$.

Thus, it could follow that there was originally nothing but invisible energy. Something then happened to start the process of this energy being transformed into matter. But where did the invisible, primordial energy come from? An answer to this is still awaited so, in the meantime, the only option seems to be to accept that it was always there.

Among those who have devised theories on how it all began, is the world-renowned physicist Stephen Hawkins. In 2010, along with co-author Leonard Mlodinow, Hawkins published a book in which he states that it is the laws of physics, not the will of God, that provides the explanation as to how the universe came into being. He adds: "it was only necessary to light the blue touch paper to set the universe going."[1] However, he does not say who lit the touch paper!

1. *The Grand Design*

The Hasidic Jewish tradition embraces a particularly appealing notion of the why, as well as the how, of creation. It is known as Contraction, or Tzimtzum theory. This was introduced to me by a Jewish academic colleague who was lecturing in transpersonal psychology, and it was further explained by Rabbi Bryks (Personal communication, vide supra).

The idea begins at a time when only God existed, and he existed everywhere. Being all-powerful, he had no needs, but he was morally benevolent and wanted to share his goodness with others. As he was everywhere, God had to contract, in order to make space for his creative light to shine. This then became the primordial dynamic of creation—he shared his goodness by creating the world. But he did not just leave it at that, he remains involved with each and every one of his people whilst, paradoxically, granting us free will.

It is time now to look in more detail at what Genesis has to say about creation, and then turn to some of the many Hebrew Scriptures that indicate widespread acceptance of this by the prophets who wrote the later narratives. Nearly all the English translations, and the Greek LXX, have, "In the beginning, God created the heavens and the earth" (Gen 1:1). Two exceptions are the *Good News* and *International Standard* versions, which prefer, "God created the universe." Interestingly, the *Wycliffe Bible* has, "God made of nought heaven and earth" (God made them out of nothing). This does rather anticipate the above discussion on what was there before the moment of creation, although it does little to resolve it!

John Gibson[2] has a lot to say about just the first two verses of the Bible. He states that verse one concerns the sovereignty of God: because he created the world he was, and remains, Lord over all things. As will be seen from the selection of references that follow, the people of Israel had to be frequently reminded to have faith in their Creator God, even through times of trial. It is noteworthy that the passage says nothing about the origin of the Almighty, but pitches straight into describing his actions. Gibson has some thoughtful observations on verse two: "Now the earth

2. *Genesis Volume 1*, 5–45.

was formless and empty, darkness was over the surface of the deep, and the spirit of God was hovering over the surface of the waters." The KJB prefers "void" to "formless," and the GNB "desolate" to "empty." In the LXX version, the Greek can be translated to mean the earth was unformed, unsightly, invisible, unfurnished, and in turmoil.

To most of us, this description of the appearance of a planet that had just been created would seem quite reasonable, and it does not clash with the scientific view.

Gibson, however, points to alternative renditions of "the spirit of God," such as the GNB's "power of God," and the original Hebrew *ruach* that can mean wind. His point is that the words could imply that the perfect God at first failed to make a perfect world; he either created the chaos that followed, or it was there in the beginning and not of his doing.

A possible explanation could be that evil was created at the same time as goodness, and the battle between the two opposites has remained ever since. It is of interest that the cosmologist's view of the origin of the universe is that almost equal quantities of two opposite elements were formed at the same time, namely matter and anti-matter.

Perhaps speculation of this nature is too fanciful, and fails to take account of the semantics of language that has been copied, edited and translated many times over the last three and a half millennia. Gibson, however, persists with his thesis, noting that the Hebrews of old realized that disorder and evil lurked behind goodness and light. For example, Isaiah quotes God as saying, "I am the Lord . . . I form the light and create darkness" (45:6–7). Thus, concludes Gibson, the first two verses of Genesis are like a gospel in embryo. They are like counterweights that are needed to create a balance between God and chaos, good and evil; we have to accept that both exist.

Following the description of the creation of the universe, the first chapter of Genesis continues by detailing the formation of the sea, land, and sky, followed by plants, animals and, finally, human beings. Whilst the order that things were created is in line with what science tells us, few take seriously the writer's statement that all this took place in just six days. The LXX Greek word is very specific: *ēmera* means day.

Most would accept the unarguable evidence from archaeology that it took many millions of years to form a habitable world. But this does not otherwise detract from the meaningfulness of the biblical version of creation, written long before the scientific age. It will be informative now to turn to just some of the many other passages that deal with matters of creation, most of which continue the theme set by the Genesis account.

In the book of Deuteronomy, Moses reminds the Israelites of their origin: "Ask now about the former days . . . from the day God created human beings" (4:32). In a later passage, which is part of what is known as "Moses' farewell song" that comprises most of chapter 32, the prophet cries, "Is this the way you repay the Lord . . . is he not your father, your creator, who made you and formed you?" (32:6). This is the first time that "father" has been used in a way that implies not just a cold, impersonal maker, but as an ancestor who remains concerned for his offspring. The Greek word *pater* in the LXX literally translates as father or progenitor.

King Hezekiah (715–686 BCE) was a faithful ruler, and one of many who acknowledged what God had done; he prayed to the Lord, "You have made heaven and earth" (2 Kgs 19:2; paralleled in Isaiah 37:16). Another faithful servant was David, who gave praise to God saying, "The Lord made the heavens" (1 Chron 16:26). Even more emphatically, a group of Levites encouraged the other Israelites to praise the Lord and say, "You made the heavens . . . (and) the earth and all that is on it . . . you give life to everything" (Neh 9:6). Job frequently affirms God's creative powers, including that he himself was a product of the Lord's hand, even though he thinks that God has abandoned him, for example, "Your hands shaped me and made me. Will you now turn and destroy me?" (10:8).

As might be expected, the book of Psalms frequently mentions the creator God. "Your heavens, the work of your fingers, the moon and stars, which you have set in place" (8:3); "The heavens are yours, and also the earth; you founded the world and all that is in it" (89:11); and, "In the beginning you laid the foundations of the earth, and the heavens are the work of your hands" (102:25), all clearly reflect the Genesis creation narrative.

Several Psalms make specific reference to living creatures, including people. For example, Psalm 104:30 states, "(All creatures look up to you) . . . When you send your spirit, they are created, and you renew the face of the ground." G. A. F. Knight[3] explains that, not only does this affirm that all living things exist because God created them, but they continue to do so by a new creative act being performed each time an individual is born. A similar message is included in Psalm 148 (5–6), although specifically in reference to human beings. The writer urges the people, "Praise the name of the Lord, for at his command they were created, and he established them for ever and ever."

Psalm 8:5 tells us something about our place in the pecking order of living things: "Human beings . . . you made them a little lower than the angels." The LXX Greek *aggelos* confirms that this text refers to divine messengers or agents of God. The next verse states that humans have been made rulers over what God has made. Thus, not only were we created as beings of high status, but we were honored by being given dominion over God's creations. As humans, we might be lower than the angels because our bodies tie us to the earth, but our spiritual souls are immortal, and thereby elevate us nearly to the level of God's messengers. But we need to be aware that being given dominion over all other living creatures is a great privilege, and we risk being deprived of this honor if we abuse it.

Further indications that the idea of a creator God was widely accepted come from Ecclesiastes (11:5) when a teacher states, "You cannot understand the work of God, the maker of all things," and Isaiah (40:28) when the prophet exclaims, "The Lord is the everlasting God, the creator of the ends of the earth." In fact Isaiah reiterates this statement many times in his book, including: "This is what the Lord says—the creator of the heavens . . . and spreads

---

3. *The Psalms, Volume 2*, 147.

out the earth" (42:5), "I the Lord have created it" (45:8), and "My own hand laid the foundations of the earth, and my right hand spread out the heavens" (48:13).

Isaiah also refers to the creation of people. In 43:7 God is reported to have said, "Everyone who is called by my name, whom I created for my glory, whom I formed and made." In similar vein: "It is I who made the earth and created mankind on it" (45:18). Isaiah himself states: "You Lord are our Father . . . we are all the work of your hand" (64:8).

Despite all efforts by prophets, kings, and others, the people of Israel often slipped back into apostasy and worshipped false gods. The Lord was both saddened and exasperated by the way the people had neglected him. In particular, he pours out his heart to Jeremiah, a prophet who dedicated his life to warning the people of the inevitable fall of Judah, if they did not turn away from apostasy. God says to Jeremiah, referring to the people of Judah, "Why have they aroused my anger with their images" (8:19), and "They go from one sin to another; they do not acknowledge me" (9:3). God then asks the prophet to say to the people, "Tell them this: 'These gods, who did not make the heavens and the earth, will perish.'"

Jeremiah himself then adds, "But God made the earth by his power . . . and stretched out the heavens by his understanding" (10:11–12). He reiterates this in 32:17 saying, "Ah, Sovereign Lord, you have made the heavens and the earth," and in 51:19 with, "For he is the maker of all things, including the people of his inheritance." Unfortunately, the prophet's warning failed to prevent the fall of Judah to the Babylonians in about 605 BCE, and the destruction of the Jerusalem temple a few years later.

Hosea is also the recipient of God's lamentations that, despite all that he has done, people are neglecting him. He says, "My people are determined to turn from me, even though they call me God most high" (11:7).

It is appropriate that the final reference to be cited with regard to creation can be found in the last book of the Hebrew Scriptures, and the verse neatly sums up what has been reported by others. Malachi says to the priests and the people of Israel, "Do we not all have one father? Did not one God create us? Why do we profane the covenant of our ancestors, by being unfaithful to one another?" (2:10).

In summary, this chapter has reviewed references to the creation of the universe, apparently out of nothing. There is a measure of agreement between the Creationists and Evolutionists on this matter, especially if the six-day time scale mentioned in Genesis is not taken literally. The many references to God as maker of all things, including people, throughout the Scriptures indicates that the original account was widely accepted. It is written that we humans were made "a little lower than the angels" and have dominion over all things, but we have an obligation to use our status responsibly. Although God made us, and is all-powerful, he is saddened when people turn away from him and revert to apostasy.

Chapter 8 ᴄᴡ

Nature Miracles

THE TOPIC OF BIBLICAL miracles often leads to one of two opposite reactions. Some people will say that they believe the events
occurred just as described in the Bible; others have the opinion
that the laws of nature cannot be changed, and that there were no
supernatural interventions or magic. Those who hold this latter
view may then lose confidence in anything the Bible states, and
even doubt that God exists. Is there a compromise explanation of
miracles that can satisfy both camps? Perhaps there is.

It may be that God *used* the laws of nature that he created
in the first place, rather than *changed* them. If this was done with
compassion, at the right time and in the right circumstances, then
he would still have been responsible for events that could have
seemed miraculous at the time. This avoids the need to accept an
unnatural cause, but does not take away divine intervention by a
loving God who cares for his people. It just remains necessary to
find explanations that fit the facts as we know them.

In order to try and discover what really happened with each
of the 35 miracles of Jesus, as reported in the New Testament,
the present writer conducted an in-depth investigation of the
evidence.[1] Firstly, the miracles were categorized as being either
a healing, exorcism, raising of the dead, or controlling nature.

1. Lowis, *The Gospel Miracles*

Secondly, judgments were made on the accuracy and reliability of the accounts, by comparing different translations, plus parallel accounts across the Synoptic Gospels where these exist.

Next, a decision was made on whether or not there could have been a naturalistic explanation for what had most likely occurred. When the narratives were first written down, the understanding of medicine, science and technology was primitive when compared with what is known today. Thus, events that could not be explained using the knowledge of the time might easily have been attributed to divine intervention.

If no naturalistic account was forthcoming, the story was then examined to see if additional evidence could have been missed at the time the event took place. Maybe a few more details could have provided a simple explanation for what happened. Finally, if the previous steps had not revealed anything significant, consideration was given to the possibility that the story was not meant to be taken literally.

Perhaps it was allegorical—with a meaning other than the obvious one. Or it could have been apocryphal—not meant to be true, but still conveying a meaningful message or lesson. Certainly Jesus told many parables that were symbolic rather than factual, in order to make his point in a way that people would understand. If the account of a miracle survived all these attempts to explain it in rational terms, then by default the only remaining explanation was a supernatural one.

It should be emphasised that this exercise was not an attempt to undermine the integrity of the biblical texts. The conclusions should not trouble those who believe that everything occurred exactly as stated, and that the miracles were acts of God, without any need to take account of the laws of nature. However, the findings might be useful to those who have previously struggled to accept that the natural order of things can be, and were, distorted by God or anyone else, in order to bring about events that otherwise might not have occurred.

The above preamble was provided because a similar approach will be taken with this current discussion on some of the miracles reported in the Hebrew Scriptures. In this chapter, some of the so-called nature miracles will be examined—events where the laws of nature were apparently overturned. In the following chapter, a selection of events dealing with healing the sick will be discussed.

We have to start with the miracle of creation itself. This has already been discussed in detail, with the conclusion that it is difficult to explain if God is left out of the picture. Chronologically, the next significant story is that of Noah and the flood, described in the seventh and eighth chapter of Genesis. John Gibson[2] devotes a considerable amount of space in his commentary to this famous story. Archaeological evidence does indeed confirm that a massive flood took place in Mesopotamia, in the region of Shuruppak, in the third or fourth millennia BCE, and several ancient traditions have similar stories of a prolonged deluge. Apparently a degree of flooding is not unusual in this area even today.

Gibson concludes that the biblical version is probably an exaggeration of what could have occurred naturally, not the least with regard to the practicalities of constructing the ark itself within the stated timescale, and the extent of the flooding. The symbolic significance of the story is that Noah represented all those who retained their faith in God when others are turning away and, because of this, he is (and therefore so also are the faithful) saved from the destruction suffered by others. There is also a warning that the Lord may choose to bring destruction to the world if humankind persists in rejecting him. We are probably safe in regarding the story of the flood not as a miracle, but as a natural event, embellished with hyperbole, and with an apocryphal significance.

The miracles of the destruction of the cities of Sodom and Gomorrah because of the sinfulness of their inhabitants, and of Lot's wife turning into a pillar of salt, are described in Genesis (19:24-26). The passage states that, "The Lord rained down burning sulphur (on the cities)," which Gibson[3] comments that today's geologists would interpret as "seismic or volcanic activity in an area of high mineral density." In that area around the Dead Sea

2. *Genesis Volume 1*
3. Ibid., 1982, 89–90.

there was not only a lot of salt but also deposits of bitumen. The seismic activity would have ignited gasses and caused an immense explosion. Lot's wife stopped to look back, and was probably caught by falling debris, incinerated, and covered with ash and mineral dust. Thus, again a natural disaster is the likely explanation, not a miracle, unless God caused this to happen just when it did.

Exodus (7:10–12) relates an amazing story. "Aaron threw down his staff . . . and it became a snake." Pharaoh's men then threw down their own staffs, and they also became snakes, but Aaron's snake swallowed up these other specimens. Whilst this achieved its purpose in demonstrating Moses and Aaron's superiority, was this really a case of transmutation, where a wooden object becomes a living creature? If this event has been accurately reported, then it is truly a case of nature being manipulated. How else might this be explained?

Could this be an optical illusion, a sleight of hand, mass hypnosis, or some other skilful illusion performed by Moses and Aaron, in order to convince the Pharaoh and his party of the superiority of their God? Snakes can become rigid when dead, and Kyle Butt[4] states that modern Egyptian magicians are adept at charming serpents. One trick is to press the nape of the snake's neck, which throws it into a cataleptic state of rigidity. It seems that the Egyptian Cobra, often depicted in the regalia and artifacts of ancient Egypt, is a suitable species for this trick.

Whilst this might be a feasible, rational explanation for the way Aaron impressed Pharaoh, there is still the matter of his snake eating all of the others. Some species can and do swallow other snakes, but it would be too much to expect one to imbibe multiple numbers of them at the same sitting. Although the NIV and GNB versions refer to the creature as a snake, the King James Bible uses serpent, as does the Greek LXX translation. The word used in the latter is *drakōn*, which literally means monstrous reptile, serpent or dragon, and a large, hungry creature such as one of these might be able to ingest several snakes in quick succession.

Despite such speculation, the whole story remains difficult to accept literally. Whether it happened as stated or not, probably the

4. *Egyptian Magicians, Snakes, and Rods*

main point to take from the narrative is that it showed the superiority of the Abrahamic God over the power that Pharaoh had to offer.

Following closely on from the snake story, is that of the plagues inflicted on Egypt because the Pharaoh would not let the Israelites leave (Ex 7:20—12:30). These have been the subject of much research, and it has been concluded that all can be explained as natural phenomena. In fact they are not uncommon in some parts of the world even today. A typical chain of events is as follows:

Turning water to blood (plague 1) can be caused by a toxic red algae that that grows in hot weather, and removes oxygen from the water. This results in fish dying, and frogs leaving the water (2). With no predators, gnats and mosquitoes flourish (3), and flies feed on the dead fish (4). Livestock dies because of the infestation, and the lack of clean water (5), and skin infections occur on people for the same reason (6). Hail is a natural phenomenon (7), and locusts swarm due to high humidity and the drought (8), also causing the skies to darken (9). Finally, firstborns could have died by being fed larger proportions of older food that was contaminated (10).[5]

Whilst explanations such as the above confirm that the laws of nature were not violated, they do not deny the possibility that the plagues occurred when they did due to divine intervention. The same applies to the well-known story of the parting of the waters, recounted in Exodus (14:21). After the 10 plagues, Pharaoh lets the Israelites leave Egypt, but later chases after them. Faced with the barrier of the Red Sea, "Moses stretched out his hand over the sea, and all that night the Lord drove the sea back with a strong east wind and turned it into dry land."

Researchers have debated where the crossing might have been. Suggestions include Lake Tanis in the Nile Delta region, a narrow part of Lake Timsah, through which the Suez Canal now passes, Nuweiba on the Gulf of Aqaba, and the northern or southern ends of the Gulf itself. The Red Sea is mentioned in another context in 1Kings (9:26). Whilst the Greek is unambiguous, the original Hebrew word translates as Reed Sea, which may have been a lake, now dried up, and located near Eliat on the northern

5. Anonymous, *http://imgur.com/gallery/x97eY*

tip of the Gulf of Aqaba. The LXX does not specifically name the sea, but does confirm the location.

Computer simulations have also shown that a strong wind is capable of blowing back the water in some of these locations, allowing a relatively dry crossing. Thus the parting of the waters can be explained as a natural occurrence, but the fortuitous timing of this event may have been more than just a mere coincidence.

Passages in Exodus (16:13) and Numbers (11:31–33) refer to the feeding of the Israelites as they journeyed through the desert. The people were complaining because they had nothing to eat. God heard their grumbling, and told Moses that he would provide what was needed. Firstly, "A wind went out from the Lord and drove quail in from the sea" (Num 11:31). Many were caught and eaten. Then, during the night, a layer of dew covered the ground. When it had dried out, there were thin flakes of a frost-like substance. This was manna, and was gathered up for food (Ex 16:13–16).

These miracles are not too difficult to explain rationally, but many believe that they occurred, or were caused to occur, by the hand of God as and when needed. Migrating quail could indeed be blown off course, and these birds often spend time on the ground, making them easy to catch. There have been several explanations for manna, including that it is the dried resin from the tamarisk tree that falls to the ground and solidifies, or perhaps crystallized honeydew from certain insects.

Numbers (17:8) relates the miraculous story of Aaron's rod budding. God informed Moses that he was going to choose a co-leader so that he would not have to bear the brunt of all the grumbling. Each of the leaders of the 12 tribes had to provide a staff to Moses, and he put these in the tent holding the Ark of the Covenant.

The next day Moses saw that the one belonging to Aaron had sprouted blossoms, buds, and had even produced almonds. Peter Naylor[6] comments that the nature of this event expressed an abundance of life, meaning that through God's chosen servant you will find life. He notes that this might explain why the word branch

6. *Numbers*, 185–6.

is referred to elsewhere in the Bible, for example, "I will make a righteous branch sprout from David's line" (Jer, 33:15).

A clue for why it was a branch specifically of an almond tree may be gleaned from other verses in Jeremiah: "The word of the Lord came to me: 'What do you see, Jeremiah?' 'I see the branch of an almond tree', I replied. The Lord said to me, 'you have seen correctly, for I am watching you to see that my word is fulfilled'" (1:11–12). A helpful footnote in the NIV Bible states that the Hebrew words for watching and almond sound alike. Thus there may be some symbolic meaning to the specifics of Aaron's rod sprouting, perhaps relating to the power of God and how he would watch the flowering of Israel.

There is little clue to inform a natural explanation for this event, unless the rod in question had been freshly cut from a healthy almond tree, and it then continued to develop. Even so, it would take longer than a day for growth to reach the level of producing fruits, and having leaves and buds all at the same time does not occur in the normal growth cycle. Cuttings of bamboo cane can grow into a new plant, given the time and appropriate conditions, as can prunings from other woody stems—but not overnight!

We do not know if the story of the sprouting almond staff is an accurate account, or was exaggerated, or was the product of trickery, perhaps by Moses to ensure that his brother Aaron was the chosen one. In view of references to it in later biblical books, however, it was obviously a significant event for the Israelites.

Two instances are described where Moses strikes a rock, which then gushes water to quench the parched thirst of the Israelites and their cattle in the desert. As was the case earlier when the people complained of lack of food, now they grumbled about the need for water. Exodus (17:6) reports that God told Moses to go to the rock at Horeb and strike it. The prophet did so, and water flowed out.

A version in Numbers (20:7–11) differs in some of the details, and opinion is divided on whether or not it is describing the same event or a different one. This time the venue is Kadesh in the desert of Zin. Moses is told to just speak to the rock, but he loses patience and forcibly strikes it twice with his staff, bringing forth water.

Because he did not do exactly what God had commanded, he was later punished by not being allowed to enter the Promised Land.

Some explorers have claimed that they have found the rock in Sinai, which shows fissures and channels where water could have once flowed, but does not do so now. Could there have been an artesian spring there all along, but the water course was blocked until an opening was created when it was struck? Alternatively, did God ignore the laws of nature, and create the flow of water? Whatever is the true cause, there has been a suggestion that this was a spiritual event, with the rock representing the Suffering Servant (Isaiah, 53:4), or the future Jesus Christ (1 Cor 10:4), from whom flows the waters of life.

One further example of a nature miracle will be given, and it relates to the fall of the walls of Jericho. This is described in Joshua (6:6–20) as a sequence of events. As conveyed to the prophet by God, on each of seven days the priests were commanded to march around outside of the city, blowing their trumpets. On the last day, when the trumpets sounded, Joshua told his army to shout loudly. The city walls then collapsed and the troops took the city. A significant point is mentioned in verse 17. Joshua orders that all living things had to be killed, except "Rehab the prostitute and all who are with her in her house . . . because she hid the spies we sent."

It has been speculated that, rather than the trumpets and shouting being powerful enough to knock down the walls, some of Joshua's men had scaled the walls and hidden in Rehab's house. When the shouting began, they emerged and broke open the city's gates from the inside. The army then entered and destroyed everything, including at least some of the walls. It was not, therefore, some miraculous power of the trumpets that enabled Jericho to be entered, but a cunning plan by Joshua. However, maybe this had been conceived by God and conveyed to the prophet.

Although there are more examples of nature miracles in the Scriptures, those reviewed here are sufficient to make the point that, in many cases, rational explanations for the events can be offered. At the risk of repetition, however, these do not exclude the hand of God being involved in them.

Chapter 9 ᖇ

Healing Miracles

THERE ARE OVER 80 references to God's healing grace in the Hebrew Scriptures, some of which will be discussed in this chapter. They commence with a very clear statement in the very first book in the Bible. Genesis (20:17) reads, "Then Abraham prayed to God, and God healed Abimelek, his wife and his female slaves so that they could have children again."

This pericope is rather a complicated one. Abraham had been spreading the story that his wife Sarah was actually his sister. This was partly true because, in reality, she was his half-sister. Neither King Abimelek's wife nor his concubines had yet produced any children. The king, hearing that Sarah was beautiful, took her into his harem. That night, in a dream, God warns Abimelek that he is a dead man because he has taken a married woman. The king protests his innocence, and says that he has not at this point had any intimate contact with Sarah. All is eventually forgiven. Sarah returns to her husband, and Abraham prays to God to remove the curse of barrenness on the king and the women of the court, which the Lord does.

Gibson[1] wonders how seriously we should take this story. Abimelek was a pagan, yet he heard and obeyed God. Sarah was an old woman, probably already pregnant with Isaac. Why should

1. *Genesis, Volume II*, 96–7.

Abraham allow his wife to be taken into the king's harem? Also, it is puzzling that God should have threatened Abimelek with punishment for an action that was done in innocence, as the king believed that Sarah was unmarried when he took her in.

Wenham[2] also queries the logic of this sequence of events, and speculates that Abraham had not manifested the same level of saintly behavior as he had done earlier. Instead he had exhibited a high level of cunning at the expense of his wife Sarah. Nevertheless God continued to protect Abraham and his followers, and he did bring about the healing that had been requested.

The question remains as to how the barrenness was overcome. Rather than accept that all the women of the harem were sterile, it would be more logical to think that the problem lay only with Abimelek himself. Just one possibility is that the king was temporarily impotent. There are various causes for male impotence and also sterility, some being physiological and others psychological. Certain drugs, diseases, excessive alcohol consumption, or physical damage can lead to impotence, as can mental states such as anxiety, guilt, or low self-esteem.

Many of these conditions can be successfully treated: diseases can be overcome, the effects of imbibing harmful substances can wear off, and anxiety can be cured. Knowing that God had forgiven him could have removed the king's feelings of guilt. If the restoring of fertility was indeed a divine act, there were many ways that God could have achieved this through natural means.

Later, in Exodus, God tells the Israelites that, if they obey his commands, he will not bring the diseases to them, as he had done to the Egyptians. He reminds them that, "I am the Lord, who heals you" (15:26), thus confirming that he has the ability to do so. Further on, Numbers (12:13–16) tells the story of how Miriam, a prophetess and leader of the Israelite women, opposed Moses and was stricken down with leprosy by God as punishment.

Despite this challenge to his leadership, Moses showed humility by crying out to God to heal Miriam. The Lord responded by telling the prophet to banish his disgraced accuser outside the

2. *Genesis*, 75.

camp for seven days. This was done, and apparently Miriam was healed. We can surmise this, firstly because it was customary for a leper to remain outside the camp as long he or she had the disease. Secondly, many years later, Micah (6:4) confirms that Miriam regained favor with God: "I brought you up out of Egypt . . . I sent Moses to lead you, and also Aaron and Miriam."

It may seem far fetched to accept that leprosy can be healed in just one week. The GNB version refers only to Miriam's skin being "suddenly covered with a dreaded disease." This is in keeping with the Greek *lepros*, which originally meant scaly or scabby skin, and not just specifically leprosy. Whilst the latter is a bacterial infection that requires extensive antibiotic treatment, other skin conditions are cured more easily. Psoriasis, for example, can be influenced by one's state of emotional well-being. Miriam's reported behavior certainly suggests that she was very agitated, so perhaps knowing that Moses had asked God to forgive her had helped her body to self-heal.

Not all reported healings are instant. In the Second Book of Kings (20:1), we read that King "Hezekiah became ill and was at the point of death." He prayed to God, professing his devotion. Isaiah was in attendance, and the Lord responded through him that he would heal the king (v. 5). On the third day Hezekiah had to go to the temple, when the Lord would than add 15 years to his life (v. 6). Isaiah gave instructions that a poultice of figs be prepared and applied to the boil, and the king recovered (v. 7). The same story is paralleled in Isaiah (38:16), which adds to the reliability of this episode.

This is the first time that the nature of the illness had been hinted at. The Greek word *elkos* can mean wound, ulcer, sore or abscess, so the problem may have been more serious than what we regard as a boil today. Such an infection might have caused septicemia that could indeed have been fatal. John Bimson[3] states that the poultice treatment was typical of the medical practices at that time, and it would have been surprising if it had not already been tried. He adds that perhaps it had, but it was ineffective until

3. *1 and 2 Kings*, 380–1.

Isaiah delivered God's promise of recovery. If this was a case of an infection that responded to treatment in three days, or longer, then it must be a naturalistic cure.

The conviction that God heals and protects is reiterated throughout the Scriptures. For example, Job's friend Eliphaz says to him, "(the Almighty) wounds, but he also binds up; he injures, but his hands also heal" (Job 5:18). This is re-stated in many psalms, such as the 41 (1–3), which is attributed to David. The king praises those who have regard for the weak: "The Lord delivers them in times of trouble . . . protects and preserves them . . . sustains them on their sick-bed and restores them . . . from illness."

˙ Somewhat more specifically, David says in Psalm 30:2, "Lord my God, I called you for help, and you healed me." In Psalm 103:2–3 he exhorts the people to, "Praise the Lord . . . and forget not his benefits—who forgives all your sins and heals all your diseases." There is a parallel to this in Jeremiah (17:14), "Heal me Lord, and I shall be healed; save me, and I shall be saved, for you are the one I praise." J. Stafford Wright[4] comments that illness [often] has its roots in wrong-living, so that the resistance of the body and mind are weakened. If we repent and seek God's forgiveness for our sins, then both our mind and body can be healed.

Today we would refer to this as holistic healing, and the link between state of mind and bodily health is well documented. Craig Keener[5] cites the interesting case of a Baptist pastor who was told that he would never speak again due to damage to his vocal chords, but suddenly regained his power of speech after reading this Psalm Was this a case of faith healing, coincidence, or divine intervention? We do not have sufficient evidence to answer this.

A similar theme is echoed in Psalm 107:171–9. Presumably referring to the Israelites after the exile, the psalmist states, "Some became fools through their rebellious ways and suffered affliction because of their iniquities . . . then they cried out to the Lord in their trouble . . . and he sent his word and healed them." G. A. F.

---

4. *Psalms*, 106.

5. *Miracles*, 495.

Knight[6] comments that here again the word-picture joins sickness and sin. Thus, when the sinfulness is overcome, then bodily healing can take place.

Just one further psalm will be mentioned: 147. Verse 3 is pertinent: "(The Lord) heals the broken-hearted and binds up their wounds." Again there is a parallel, this time in Isaiah (61:1), "The Lord has anointed me to proclaim good news to the poor. He has sent me to bind up the broken-hearted." The scenario refers to the return of the exiles from Babylon, along with others who were persecuted or scattered, and the rebuilding of Jerusalem.

The Jews had experienced an unhappy time in exile, and were trickling back to their homeland with an air of despondency. God is aware of their needs. Despite the fact that they had at least partly brought their banishment on themselves through apostasy, God still cares for them as he had always promised to do. He therefore heals their despair, and treats their wounds.[7]

Turning now to the book of Proverbs, which contains many words of wisdom, three references to healing will be mentioned. In chapter 3:7–8 we read of the exhortation to, "Do not be wise in your own eyes; fear the Lord and shun evil. This will bring health to your body and nourishment to your bones." This is a good example of taking responsibility for your own health by living a good life. In keeping with what has been said already regarding the link between the mind and body, Keener[8] comments that some recoveries stem from emotional or mental cures, both through strengthening the body's immune response, or by addressing the psychological roots of a physical illness. The Proverbs writer then passed on his many words of wisdom to his sons, saying, "Pay attention to what I say . . . for they are life to those who find them and health to one's whole body" (4:20–22). Many would no doubt agree with this statement.

Solomon, or whoever it was who wrote this book, was very astute in anticipating what medical science has discovered only

6. *The Psalms, Volume 2*, 167.
7. Wright, *Psalms*, 148.
8. *Miracles*, 630.

relatively recently. In my book on the Gospel miracles[9] I mentioned Sigmund Freud's theory of hysterical neurosis. This holds that emotional traumatic events can be repressed, and converted into neurological symptoms. These in turn can be converted to a range of physical conditions including paralysis, interference with vision, hearing, and speech, and fainting. Where a condition has a psychological origin, then a faith cure can heal it. This process is often referred to as psychoneuroimmunology (PNI), which describes the link between emotion, brain function, and the immune response that can fight physical illness.

The Proverbs quotation from chapter three, cited above, changes the emphasis from a faith cure by another, to righteous living that can help keep both body and mind healthy. There is an even more specific example of this in 17:22, namely, "A cheerful heart is good medicine, but a crushed spirit dries up the bones." What can be more specific than this—being miserable can make you physically ill, but being cheerful keeps you healthy!

Isaiah provides many reassurances that the Almighty cares for us. For example, in 35:4 he urges the people to "Be strong, do not fear; your God will come . . . he will come to save you." In the year 722 BCE the Assyrians had conquered the northern kingdom of Israel, and taken the 10 tribes into captivity. They were then proving to be a threat to the Judean exiles. The people were also wondering if the promised Messiah would ever come. Isaiah's message is that they should not be despondent, but must remain strong. He reassures them that God will indeed come to their aid, and his words anticipate the birth of the Savior, Jesus Christ, some 700 years later.

Further on, in 53:5, Isaiah proclaims that the servant, "Was pierced for our transgressions, he was crushed for our iniquities . . . and by his wounds we are healed." This sounds very much as if Isaiah was again prophesising about the future, and the fate of Jesus when he came as the Messiah. If this was not the writer's intention, then who was the servant? Derek Kidner[10] is not the only

9. Lowis, *The Gospel Miracles*, 26–7.

10. *Isaiah*, 657–63.

commenter who regards this as a reference to the nation of Israel, whose people had to endure suffering at the hands of oppressors.

This argument is strengthened by three earlier passages in Isaiah known as Servant Songs, all obviously relating to Israel. The passage from chapter 53 quoted above is regarded by many as song number four. Isaiah continues the theme of helping his chosen people, this time by pledging to heal those whose apostasy has brought the nation to destruction: "I have seen their ways, but I will heal them; I will guide them and restore comfort to Israel's mourners" (57:18).

Jeremiah, who had warned the people of Judah of destruction if they did not turn from sin, feels despondent that his words had failed to convince the people. He needs comforting himself, and he prays confidently to God, "Heal me, Lord, and I shall be healed; save me and I shall be saved, for you are the one I praise" (17:14). Later, he writes to try and encourage the exiles not to give up hope, and assures them that God has not abandoned them, even though they need to pay for their apostasy. The prophet quotes the Lord as saying, "I will discipline you but only in due measure; I will not let you go entirely unpunished" (30:11). He continues, "But I will restore you to health and heal your wounds" (v. 17).

In chapter 33:6 Jeremiah repeats God's promise that, despite what has happened, he will restore the nation by bringing health and healing to it. A similar message was given to the Israelites much earlier, when the Lord promised to keep them free of the same plagues that he inflicted on the Egyptians. However, this was on condition that they kept all his commands and decrees (Ex 15:26, vide supra).

We are nearing the end of this trawl through the Hebrew Scriptures to identify some of the many references that attest to God's healing work, and just three more will be cited. Two passages in Hosea continue with the promise that Israel has sinned, but will be forgiven and restored. Firstly, in chapter 6:1 it is stated, "Come, let us return to the Lord. He has torn us to pieces but he will heal us; he has injured us but will bind up our wounds."

The second is a little more cryptic: "It was I who taught Ephraim to walk . . . but they did not realize it was I who healed them" (11:3). The reason why the single name "Ephraim" is followed by the plural "them" is because the tribe of Ephraim was often taken to represent the whole of the northern kingdom of Israel that was conquered by Assyria. This verse has parallels elsewhere in the Scriptures, for example, "But I will restore you to health and heal your wounds" (Jer 30:17), and "The Lord binds up the bruises of his people and heals the wounds he inflicted" (Isa 30:26).

This enquiry into evidence of God's healing grace commenced with a passage from Genesis, the first book in the Bible, and it is perhaps fitting that the final extract is from Malachi, the last of the Hebrew Scriptures. In the ultimate chapter of this book, the prophet quotes the Lord as saying that, on the day when he acts, the evildoers will be set on fire, "But for you who revere my name, the sun of righteousness will rise with healing in its rays" (4:2). John James[11] comments that the righteous will know the warmth and healing of salvation, and that it will be a day of ultimate blessing for the people of God.

To summarize what has been found regarding one aspect of what God does, namely healing, we have a range of examples that appear throughout the Scriptures, from the very beginning to the very end. Thus, it is obviously a recurring act of God that was highly regarded by most of the Scripture writers. In the earlier books there are examples of individuals who have been healed, for example Abimelek, Miriam, and Hezekiah. Then there are many statements that indicate a conviction that God heals and protects, including several in Psalms. These are often linked to the need to repent from sin, and they involve a holistic healing of both mind and body.

Most of the healings mentioned in the later books refer to the healing of nations rather than individuals. First the northern kingdom of Israel, and then the southern nation of Judah, were invaded and many inhabitants taken into captivity. These events occurred because of the unfaithfulness and apostasy of the people,

11. *Haggai, Zechariah and Malachi*, 164.

who were then punished for their sins. However, this situation would not last forever, because God had pledged never to permanently abandon his Chosen People. It was left to prophets such as Jeremiah to try and maintain hope and optimism among those banished from their homelands. The writers gave assurances that one day their nations will be restored, and that God will bring them health and healing.

Chapter 10 ᦇ

God's Laws

GOD MADE MANY LAWS, and most of them are listed in the first five books of the Bible: Genesis, Exodus, Leviticus, Numbers, and Deuteronomy, collectively known as the Pentateuch, Torah, or the Laws of Moses. In total there are 613 of them, which can be grouped into 248 positives (the do's) with 18 subsections, and 365 negatives (the don'ts) with 13 subsections[1].

The book containing the most laws is Leviticus, with nearly 39 per cent of the total. These are dominated by requirements concerning the temple and the priests, including many relating to sacrifices. There are also prohibitions regarding agriculture, and forbidden relationships such as incest. Deuteronomy contains about 34 per cent of the laws. These are particularly concerned with the relationship with God, idolatry, community, social, and family matters, and the negatives resulting from historical events such as fraternizing with those who were enemies.

Almost 20 per cent of the do's and don'ts are found in Exodus, including those relating to legal requirements and justice, the treatment of slaves, festivals, and temple requirements. The book of Numbers contains relatively few laws, but it exclusively lists rules concerning the treatment of the Nazarites—a sect whose

---

1. Anonymous, "God's word first," *http://gods-word-first.org/bible-study/ 613commandments.html).*

members had taken a vow of abstinence. Genesis contains only two requirements, both relating to family matters.

The categories mentioned above are not necessarily restricted to a single book, and some specific topics are mentioned in more than one of them. For example, the 10 Commandments appear in both Exodus (20:2–17) and Deuteronomy (5:6–21). The list of 613 laws only includes one citation of each, but the parallel accounts mean that the do's and don'ts feature more times than this throughout the Pentateuch.

The presence of so many requirements begs the question: why did God impose all these on the Israelites? Two salient points impinge on any attempt to answer this. The first is, was it actually God who created these decrees, or was a human hand involved in at least some of them? Secondly, what was the situation at the time these laws were conveyed to the people (the *Sitz im Leben*)? Although pious Jews today still try to follow as many of the requirements as possible, we are not living in the second millennium BCE and, therefore, it may be questioned whether or not at least some of them are still necessary.

With regard to the question of the origin of the numerous laws, we are on fairly solid ground if we start with the Decalogue. According to the two accounts we have, the Commandments were conveyed to Moses directly by God, on Mount Sinai. The first four concern the divine/human relationship. The Lord had chosen his people, and rescued them from Egypt. He had made a covenant with them, promising to bless and protect them as his Chosen People. However, in return they had to be obedient to his law and be faithful to him alone.

He stated that they must have no God but him, must not worship idols, nor use his name in vain, and must keep the Sabbath holy. The remaining six Commandments apply to relationships between the people themselves. They prohibit murder, theft, adultery, making false accusations, and desiring another man's wife or possessions. Finally, there is an exhortation to respect one's parents. It can be argued that not all of these are laws as such, and only two of them—killing and stealing—are criminal offences in modern law courts. The other four relate to desirable ethical behavior that should result in harmonious social community living.

If we have reliable evidence from the texts that the 10 Commandments came directly from God, what about the remaining 603 laws? It may help to concentrate on the evidence from just one of the books—Deuteronomy. This comprises 956 verses, but only 21 quotations, totaling some 77 verses, appear to be the direct words of God. The first 16 are preceded by Moses stating, "The Lord said to me" (example 1:42) or similar, followed by a verbatim statement. The remaining five instances commence with words such as, "The Lord said to Moses" (such as 31:14), as if written by a narrator, which is then followed by a statement of what was said.

In total, God's direct contribution makes up only about eight per cent of the whole book. In addition, there are a few instances of reported speech where Moses states, "Then the Lord told me" (e.g. 2:2), or similar, as well as the prophet speaking on behalf of God, such as, "The Lord will bless you" or "curse you" (see examples in Deuteronomy chapter 28). The point being made here is that the vast majority of Deuteronomy comprises Moses' own words, and it is not always made clear how many of the numerous regulations were actually conveyed to him by God.

During the discussion in chapter 4 concerning the origins of the Hebrew Scriptures, some doubts were expressed about the authorship of the Pentateuch. Whilst it is traditionally regarded as the work of Moses, writing somewhere in the thirteenth to fifteenth centuries BCE, even conservative scholars accept that some passages indicate later additions. In Deuteronomy, for example, the book commences with, "These are the words Moses spoke to all Israel . . . east of the Jordan" (1:1), which suggests they may have been penned by a narrator. The final chapter, 34, concerns the death of Moses, so it obviously could not have been written by the prophet himself.

M. E. Biddle[2] notes that the reference to "east of the Jordan," which is repeated in verse 5 of the same chapter, implies that somebody wrote these words once the Israelites had already

2. *Deuteronomy*

crossed over to the west bank. From this and other evidence, it is quite possible that the original text has been revised, edited, and added to several times during the 3,000 or more years since it was written. In addition to this, as with all biblical manuscripts, there is also the matter of the errors that could have occurred during the numerous copyings and translations that have taken place before the publishing of the modern versions available to us today.

To return to the question of whether God himself was responsible for creating all the 613 laws, the doubts already discussed can be supplemented by the answer to the second question: what was the situation at the time the text was written? The Israelites were on a journey to the Promised Land, which was to last all of 40 years. It is understandable that they would become impatient, and even rebellious, over this time. They faced many hazards, sometimes including shortages of food or water. There would have been squabbles over leadership, family ties may have broken and, even more relevant, there were doubts about God and his promises.

Indeed, there is more than one example of the people turning to apostasy and worshiping false gods. Exodus chapter 32 tells the story of the golden calf, Numbers (25:3) contains the first mention of bowing down to Baal, whilst Deuteronomy describes Moses warning the people to avoid the temptation to worship other gods (11:16), and to destroy the shrines where this is seen in other lands (12:2). If the Israelites were to have any hope of entering the Promised Land and succeeding in establishing themselves, it was vital that they remain united, and faithful to the one God.

The reason for laboring the question about the authorship of the laws is that, if they all originated directly from God, then it would give the impression of him being a deity who ruled by fear, prescribed extremely cruel punishments, and who manipulated human beings simply for his own pleasure and self-satisfaction. Some examples of these draconian laws will be given shortly. Is this what God is really like?

An alternative view is that Moses created most of the laws himself, as and when they were needed, although he grouped them around common themes, each based on one of the 10

Commandments.[3] When the Israelites were on the verge of entering the hostile Promised Land, they comprised a loose confederation of tribes needing to be united. They were also about to be exposed to the apostasy of the Canaanites and those who would be their neighbors. In order to prepare the people for this, it was necessary to establish systems to regulate both secular and religious activities.[4]

Some of the procedures and punishments included among the laws are so extreme and barbaric that it would be surprising if they were all carried out at the time, and certainly not in the present day. More than 120 of the 613 are concerned with the sacrificing of animals. This was a common event throughout the period of the Hebrew Scriptures, and into at least the first century of the New Testament. It only ceased to be widespread when the Jerusalem temple was destroyed in 70 CE, so that there was no appointed place for the sacrifices to take place. Also, for Christians at least, Jesus offering himself as the sacrificial lamb eliminated the need for physical sacrifices to continue.[5] It is, however, still practiced in some countries even today, and the ritual slaughter of animals for food is obligatory in Jewish and Islamic communities.

Animal sacrifices were carried out for a variety of reasons, as detailed in the first few chapters of Leviticus. All animals had to be perfect in every way, and the one bringing the offering had to lay a hand on the animal to symbolize that the beast was taking the person's place as it was being killed. There were burnt offerings to celebrate morning, evening, the Sabbath, childbirth, and various festivals. Then there were peace offerings were the meat could be eaten. Other types of sacrifice include sin offerings and guilt offerings, often accompanied by detailed rituals that included blood sprinkling.

To the non-adherent, these practices may seem to be a waste of good food, especially when this may not have been plentiful, and a relatively easy way for a person to absolve themselves from

3. Walton, *Deuteronomy*, 213–5.

4. Butler, *Holman Concise Bible Dictionary*, 160–1.

5. Ibid., 347–9.

their transgressions. They can also be seen to cause unnecessarily suffering to the animals themselves. This also applies to some of the other laws involving animals. The first nine verses of Deuteronomy chapter 21 describe an elaborate ritual to be carried out when there was an unsolved murder. A heifer that had never been worked had to be taken to a valley that had not been planted, and have its neck broken. The elders were to then wash their hands over the animal, and declare that they were innocent of the crime. This was regarded as an atonement for the people of Israel. The passage does not state what then happened to the unfortunate dead animal.

Although not given as a law, Genesis (15:1–21) describes how God gave Abraham instructions to take a heifer, goat and ram, each three years old, plus a dove and a pigeon. He was to cut each of the three larger animals in half and lay them in rows. Abraham then went to sleep, and had a vision that a smoking brazier and flaming torch passed between the pieces of flesh. These items presumably represented the deity, and this apparently confirmed the covenant that God had made with the prophet.[6] This story is referred to in Jeremiah (34:18–21). Leviticus (5:6–9) states the need for a person to bring a female lamb or goat for sacrifice as an atonement for sinning. If they cannot afford these animals, they are to bring two doves or pigeons, and the priest will wring the head off the neck of one of them.

To be fair, there are also laws that deal with animal welfare, for example, "If you see the donkey of someone who hates you fallen down under its load, do not leave it there, be sure you help them with it" (Ex 23:5). Similarly, Deuteronomy (22:4) reads, "If you see your fellow Israelite's donkey or ox fallen in the road, do not ignore it. Help the owner to get it to its feet."

A rather more dubious benefit to the creature is described in the chapter that follows (22:6–7). It concerns finding a bird's nest with the mother and young: "You may take the young, but be sure to let the mother go." Finally, 25:4 of the same books states, "Do not muzzle an ox while it is treading grain." Whilst this appears to

6. Gibson, *Genesis, Volume ll*, 54.

relate to allowing the beast to eat whilst it is working, there may be allegorical implications for people being allowed to partake of the fruits of their labors.

Despite a few examples of this nature, most of the evidence, especially relating to sacrifices, suggests that animal welfare may not have been an over-riding consideration. However, it was not only animals that forfeited their lives, but capital punishment was advocated for a surprising range of human transgressions, some of which seem relatively minor today. Deuteronomy states that if your very own brother, son, daughter or wife entices you to worship other gods, "You must certainly put them to death . . . your hand must be the first . . . stone them to death" (13:6–10).

A few chapters further on the writer states that, if someone has a stubborn and rebellious son, his parents must take him to the town's gate, and "Then all the men of his town are to stone him to death" (21:21). Parallel, although slightly different, versions of these laws that relate to the need to respect parents are found in Exodus, chapter 21, which also states the ruling, "Anyone who kidnaps someone is to be put to death" (verse 16).

It was particularly hard being a woman in this patriarchal society. According to Exodus (23:18), the law states, "Do not allow a sorceress to live." If a man accuses his new bride of not being a virgin, and the woman cannot prove that she was, "She shall be brought to the door of her father's house and there the men of the town shall stone her to death" (Deut 22:21).

Although there is no law that requires men to be similarly chaste, they sometimes had to pay a penalty for their philandering. If a man meets in a town a virgin pledged to be married, and sleeps with her, they both have to die—the woman because she did not cry out. If this happens in the country, only the man is put to death, because the woman's screams could not be heard (ibid 25, 27).

To cite just one final example of extreme punishment, Deuteronomy (13:13–15) describes what to do if you hear that troublemakers have led the people astray, and encouraged them to worship false gods. If a thorough investigation shows that this is true, then, "You must certainly put to the sword all who live in that town. You must destroy it completely, both its people and its livestock." One may be excused for asking "Why?"

What can be concluded about God, the lawgiver? Did he really create all 613 laws, and expect that they would be relevant for all time? If this were indeed the case, then we can understand how some people think that the Almighty was all-controlling, and at times manipulative, misogynist, and oblivious of the suffering caused to humans and animals when trying to comply with all the requirements. The relevance of the situation at the time the Scriptures were written has already been mentioned. It was vital that the loose confederation of tribes that were the Israelites, remain united and strong as they completed their 40 year journey and prepared to enter the Promised Land. Squabbles, even within families, would weaken the ability for them to succeed in their mission.

Once established in Canaan, governmental, judicial and social systems would have to be established to help the new nation survive and prosper. Thus, a strong code of living was needed, although it could be argued that the need for many of the specific laws would fall away once a stable society was established. It may have been that the laws were not intended to be taken literally, and that the threat of harsh punishment was expected to be a deterrent. John Walton[7] suggests that the structure of Deuteronomy is designed to elucidate the broader morality behind the Decalogue. The so-called laws were not a set of restrictive rules, but were rather principles and guidance for living life as the People of God.

Perhaps we can have confidence that God did indeed create the 10 Commandments, to which few can object, but we do not know how much influence God had on the many requirements presented by Moses. About 3,000 years have passed since the laws were created, and the challenges facing life today suggest the need for some selectivity in deciding which of the 613 are still relevant.

7. *Deuteronomy*, 213–5.

Chapter 11 ᴄᴎ

Judgment and Punishment

IN MOST SOCIETIES, THE responsibility for maintaining order and harmonious social structure is divided between three independent bodies. One, the legislators, make the laws, the executive then ensures that the laws are enforced and the perpetrators caught, and the judiciary decides whether or not a crime has been committed and, if so, what the sentence should be.

The previous chapter identified 613 laws that either came from God, or were formulated on earth at the time to suit the situation then pertaining (the SIL). Although alleged breaches of these laws were heard by the elders or local judges, the Scriptures include more than 80 texts that have either God himself stating that he is the ultimate judge, or others declaring that this is the case. In addition, there are at least 60 citations relating how the Lord punishes transgressors, this being mainly for apostasy.

The references to judgment start in Genesis, chapter 3, when God finds out that Adam and Eve had eaten from the tree of knowledge. It continues in 6:5 when, "The Lord saw how great the wickedness of the human race had become on earth." It is clear that, even from the earliest of times, the people accepted that the Almighty was the final arbitrator of all things. In chapter 18:25, Abraham asks God the rhetorical question, "Will not the judge of all the earth do right?" He was enquiring whether or not the Lord will spare Sodom if a number of righteous people are found there, although he also implied that he will accept the outcome whatever it was. The final mention in the first book of the Bible concerns Laban, brother of Rebekah, who was in dispute with Jacob. He exclaims, "May the God of Abraham and the God of Nahor, the God of their father, judge between us" (31:53).

One of many examples of God judging that the people had become unfaithful to him occurs in Joshua (7:11) when he declares to the prophet, "Israel has sinned; they have violated my covenant, which I commanded them to keep." It is appropriate that at least one acknowledgement of who is responsible for the big decisions is found in the book of Judges itself. In chapter 11:27, Jephthah the Gileadite sent a message to the Ammonite king, who had fought with the people of Israel rather than let them pass through his country. He said, "Let the Lord, the Judge, decide the dispute this day between the Israelites and the Ammonites."

Likewise Hannah, wife of Elkanah and mother of the prophet Samuel prays to God saying, "The Lord will judge the ends of the earth" (1 Sam 2:10). Even the powerful King David instructed his priests to praise God, exclaiming, "Let the trees of the forest sing, let them sing for joy before the Lord, for he comes to judge the earth" (1 Chron 16:33).

An interesting variation on this theme occurs in the Second Book of Chronicles (19:6). Jehoshaphat, king of Judah, appoints judges but then tells them, "Consider carefully what you do, because you are not judging for mere mortals but for the Lord, who is with you whenever you give a verdict." Thus, apparently even fallible human judges are responsible to God for their decisions. This is in keeping with the decree laid down in Deuteronomy that the Israelites shall, "Appoint judges and officials for each of your tribes . . . and they shall judge the people fairly" (16:18). Job makes it clear that the decision of the Almighty is final, and laments, "How can I find words to argue with him . . . though I were innocent . . . I could only plead with my judge for mercy" (8:14–15).

The Psalms often sing praises to God's actions and attributes, and that of judgment is no exception. Psalm 7, attributed to David, exclaims, "Let the Lord judge the peoples" (verse 8), and "God is a righteous judge" (verse 11). David repeats this affirmation in 9:4, and another writer, Asaph, expresses with confidence, "It is God who judges" (75:7), and "Rise up, O God, and judge the earth" (82:8). The message continues in Psalm 96, "The Lord . . . will judge people with equity" (verse 10), and "He comes to judge the earth" (verse 13). The same message is repeated elsewhere, but we can give the final quotation to David, "The Lord . . . will judge nations" (110:6). Thus, the psalm writers leave us in no doubt where they think the ultimate judicial authority lies.

Isaiah also makes several mentions of this. He has a vision, and describes what he saw, including what will happen in the last days. He says that, "The law will go out from Zion, the word of the Lord from Jerusalem. He will judge between the nations and will settle disputes for many peoples" (2:3–4). Derek Kidner[1] explains that the people at that time had a need of God's uncompromising truth and rule. Lamenting what the unbelievers have done to bring ruination to the nation at the hands of the Assyrians, Isaiah says, "The Lord takes his place in court; he rises to judge the people. The Lord enters into judgment against the elders and leaders of the people" (3:13–14). But then confidence that salvation is at hand returns. In a very long song of praise, Isaiah says, "For the Lord is our judge, the Lord is our lawgiver, the Lord is our king; it is he who will save us" (33:22).

The people of Judah had broken the covenant and plotted against Jeremiah, but God had revealed the plot to him. Gordon McConville[2] points out that Jeremiah was already complaining of his suffering, resulting from him being called as a prophet in the first place. The plot against him was particularly distressing because it was hatched by people of his own town, possibly because of his criticism of the temple establishment. The prophet was seeking vindication, and prayed to God, "But you, Lord Almighty, who judge righteously . . . let me see your vengeance on them" (11:20).

1. *Isaiah*, 65.
2. *Jeremiah*, 683.

God reassures Jeremiah that he will keep his original promise to be with him, and rescue him in times of trouble (1:17–18).

Ezekiel reports what the Lord had said to him about the punishment to be meted out to sinful Israel: "The end is now upon you . . . I will judge you according to your conduct" (7:3). He repeats this in verse 27 and then in several other subsequent passages. The final mention occurs after the threatened destruction has taken place. God reports retrospectively on his earlier judgment: "I dealt with them according to their uncleanness and their offences, and I hid my face from them" (39:24).

Finally, with respect to the judgment role of God, the Minor Prophets reiterate the earlier messages. Joel (3:12) envisages the coming Day of the Lord when the nations that have opposed him will be punished. He conveys God's word to, "Let the nations be roused; let them advance into the Valley of Jehoshaphat, for there I will sit to judge all the nations on every side." (3:12). What is almost a parallel text is found in Micah (4:3), concerning the last days. The prophet reports that, (the Lord) "Will judge between many peoples and will settle disputes for strong nations far and wide."

The presence of so many verses in the Scriptures, penned over about 1,000 years, pertaining to God being the ultimate judge must be significant. It emphasizes widespread acceptance of the authority of the Almighty as the undisputed arbitrator of all things. Perhaps this was linked with the belief that the Lord also had the power to punish both individuals and whole nations if he found them guilty, especially of being unfaithful. It is to examples of such punishments that we now turn, whilst the chapter that follows will discuss the good things that happen to those who remain faithful to the one God.

The references made earlier to the consequences of breaking some of the laws, and also the wanton destruction of whole towns that occurred in the case of Sodom and Jericho, show that the Lord's punishments could be very severe indeed. Are those who believe in the God of Abraham happy to worship a deity who appears to be responsible for so much wanton slaughter of both humans and animals? We can be informed by a selective trawl through the Scriptures to see what is written about God's punishment.

References to punishments start with those given to Adam and Eve for eating the forbidden fruits (Gen 3:16–24). These included painful childbearing for the woman, and hard work plus banishment for the man. Sudden fire from the altar caused the death of Aaron's sons Nadab and Abihu, because they defied instructions and brought their own burning incense container to the holy place (Lev 10:1–2). God then reels off a long list of punishments for disobedience (26:14–39). These include disease, defeat by enemies, barren soil for crops, attack by wild animals, plague, famine, and even eating the flesh of one's sons and daughters. It is not known if these threats were carried out in all their gory detail!

The writer of Deuteronomy reminds the people of God's prerogative to punish those who are unfaithful: "From heaven he made you hear his voice to discipline you" (4:36). Likewise, "As a man disciplines his son, so the Lord your God disciplines you" (8:5). The final chapter describes the death of Moses who, despite all his trials and tribulations in leading the Israelites to the Promised Land, was not himself allowed to enter it (chapter 34). This was due to one discretion, reported in Numbers (20, 9–12), where he struck the rock to bring forth water, instead of just speaking to it. This seems very harsh treatment for one of God's most loyal and hard-working servants.

The prophet Samuel gives some examples of what God can do, when he reproduces his mother's prayer: "The Lord brings death and makes alive; he brings to the grave and raises up . . . (he) sends poverty and wealth; he humbles and exalts" (1 Sam 2:6–7). Job's colleague, Eliphaz, also indicates his acceptance of the Lord's authority when he states, "Blessed is the one whom God corrects; so do not despise the discipline of the Almighty" (Job 5:17). However, Samuel then describes the severe penalty inflicted on Uzzah, just for touching the ark when the oxen stumbled: "God struck him down, and he died there beside the ark of God" (2 Sam, 6:7, paralleled in 1 Chron, 13:9).

The psalmists acknowledged the authority of the Lord to judge, forgive, or punish, sometimes for a person's own good. For example, "Blessed is the one you discipline, Lord, the one you teach from your law; you grant them relief from their days of trouble" (94:12–13). There is uncertainty about the author and circumstances of Psalm 118, which includes the words, "The Lord has chastened me severely, but has not given me over to death" (verse 18). This could refer to the promise conveyed by Nathan to David that God would make his name great, as described in 2 Samuel (7:8–11). If this were the case, it would date the psalm to around 1,000 BCE, when the king was reviewing how his life had been protected and nurtured by God. Another possibility is that it could refer to the return of the exiles from the Southern Kingdom in 539 BCE, with the personal pronoun "me" representing the nation as a whole. It would confirm that God had eventually forgiven the people for their apostasy.

Psalm 145, attributed to David, continues the message of reward or punishment. Verse 20 reads, "The Lord watches over all who love him, but all the wicked he will destroy." The same theme is later taken up by David's son, Solomon: "My son, do not despise the Lord's discipline, and do not resent his rebuke, because the Lord disciplines those he loves, as a father the son he delights in" (Prov 3:11–12). Likewise, in 23:13 he writes, "Do not withhold discipline from a child; if you punish them with the rod, they will not die." Clearly, the message is that such chastisement is good for you, and helps you to learn the way of righteousness.

As usual, Isaiah makes a contribution, this time with a report of a vision he had experienced. The Southern Kingdom of Judah was being threatened by Assyria, which had already conquered Israel to the north; it was also risking its internal destruction through apostasy. The prophet's message to the people was, "The day of the Lord is coming . . . I (God) will punish the world for its evil, the wicked for their sins" (13:9, 13). He then spells out some details of this punishment: the sun, moon and stars will not show any light, the heavens will tremble and the earth will shake. In addition, people will flee, but whoever is caught will fall by the sword, and their infants will be dashed to pieces. Once angered, this shows that God intended to punish sinners most severely. But why should the innocent infants also suffer?

Isaiah later repeats his message, "See the Lord is coming . . . to punish the people of the earth for their sins" (26:21). The reaction of the population to this is reported as: "The sinners of Zion are terrified; trembling grips the godless" (33:14). The prophet then makes it clear what is shortly to take place: "See, the Lord is coming with fire, and his chariots are like a whirlwind; he will bring down his anger with fury" (66:15). History reports that the Babylonians conquered Judah in 597 BCE, and destroyed Jerusalem and its temple 11 years later. God always promised that he would forgive the people once they had been punished, and the Judeans were allowed to return to their homeland in 539 BCE.

Jeremiah had devoted his life to trying to prevent the Southern Kingdom from succumbing to sinfulness, but his efforts had been in vain. He addressed the people, quoting the Almighty as saying to the people of Judah, "Your wickedness will punish you; your backsliding will rebuke you. Consider then and realise how evil and bitter it is for you when you forsake the Lord your God" (2:19). Jeremiah had urged the king to surrender to Babylon and thus avoid bloodshed, but his counsel was ignored. Later, in a last-ditch attempt to avoid destruction, King Zedekiah asks Jeremiah to intercede with God on his behalf. However, the Lord rejects this plea, saying, "I will punish you as your deeds deserve" (21:14).

The prophet is clearly upset about Judah's fate. He says, "Your own conduct and actions have brought this on you. This is your punishment. How bitter it is! How it pierces to the heart! Oh my anguish, my anguish! I writhe in pain" (4:18–19). When a plot against Jeremiah is uncovered, the Lord tells him, "I will punish them (i.e. the plotters). Their young men will die by the sword, their sons and daughters by famine" (11:22). Thus, once again God's punishment extends beyond the actual perpetrators, which seems unduly harsh. After the invasion, the prophet was spared because of his efforts to make peace but not so King Zedekiah, who had his eyes put out and his sons executed.

Jeremiah is believed to have also written the book of Lamentations, and he too wondered if the penalties inflicted on the Judeans were over-zealous. He writes, "Look Lord, and consider: whom have you ever treated like this? Should women eat their offspring? . . . Should priest and prophet be killed? . . . No one escaped or survived; those I cared for and reared my enemy has destroyed" (Lam 2:20–22). But a little later he seems to have accepted what has happened: "Why should the living complain when punished for their sins?" (3:39). Nevertheless, the writer still laments that: "The punishment of my people is greater than that of Sodom" (4:6). To compare Jerusalem with Sodom is quite profound, as the latter's wickedness justified the destruction that befell it.[3]

The priest Ezekiel was one of the many people of Judah who, following the invasion, was exiled to Babylon. In contrast to previous punishments meted out to whole communities, including women and children, in his short book the opposite is stated: "The one who sins is the one who will die. The child will not share the guilt of the parent, nor will the parent share the guilt of the child" (Ezek 18:20). Whilst this seems fair, we can be forgiven for asking why this has not always been the case? Whatever the answer, God still needs to remind people that he is both judge and enforcer. Ezekiel quotes the Lord as saying, "I will display my glory among the nations, and all the nations will see my punishment" (39:21).

God's punishment of Israel for its unfaithfulness continues to be mentioned in later books. Hosea states that God had said, "The days of punishment are coming" (9:7), and "When I please, I will punish them" (10:10). More specifically, Amos adds, "I will send fire on Judah" (2:4). Malachi (4:1) refers to the unsatisfactory behaviour of the priests: "Surely the day is coming; it will burn like a furnace. All the arrogant and every evildoer will be stubble." God would send Elijah to help them reform but, if this did not succeed, he says, "I will come and strike the land with total destruction" (4:5).

As with the judgements, the earlier references to punishment deal mainly with that meted out to individuals, whilst the later

3. McConville, *Lamentations,* 714.

ones tend to relate to sanctions against Israel and Judah for failing to keep their side of the covenant obligations. The warnings and exhortations of many prophets go unheeded. Some of the punishments do seem to be severe, especially when they include whole families or communities, regardless of individual differences. However, assurances are given that God will eventually forgive his chosen people, and let them return to their Promised Land.

Chapter 12 ～

Rewards for the Faithful

WHY SHOULD THERE BE so many references to reward and punishment in the Scriptures? In many cases these relate to the covenants made by God, which required both the originator and recipients to honor their respective obligations. Whereas the Lord was able to keep his side of the contract, human beings often failed to do likewise.

Covenants resemble suzerain treaties that were common in biblical times. Often these were made between a king or other ruler (the suzerain) who had the power to protect the people (the vassals), and the subjects who, in return, had to comply with various obligations that acknowledged the superiority of the overlord. These treaties could be either equal, with benefits to both parties, or unequal where all the advantages were with the superior power to whom another party might have surrendered.

C. J. H. Wright[1] provides a useful exposition of the covenants described in the Bible. Although some say that such a treaty was made with Adam, that with Noah (Gen 9:8–17) is generally acknowledged to be the first. God sent the flood to punish the people for their wickedness. Afterwards, he promises unilaterally not to destroy the earth and its inhabitants, and the rainbow would

---

1. *The Mission of God*

be a sign of this. No obligations were placed on Noah and his descendents in return.

Next is the covenant with Abraham, which is first mentioned in Genesis chapters 12 and 15. The Lord recognized Abraham as being a faithful and righteous person. He tells him that he will have many descendents, and they will be given land. More details are given in chapter 19 (verses 1–11), with the promise of the territory of Canaan. This time there was a condition: all the males now and in the future had to be circumcised, as a sign of the covenant between them. Although covenants are generally regarded as applying only to the chosen people of Israel, when Abraham demonstrates his obedience by preparing to sacrifice Isaac, God said to him, "Through your offspring all the nations on earth will be blessed" (Gen 22:18).

Perhaps the most frequently quoted treaty is that between God and Moses made on Mount Sinai, as spelled out in Exodus (19:3–6). The Lord said that the Israelites would be his Chosen People. They would be: "A Kingdom of priests and a holy nation" (19:6). There was, however, a condition. The people had to obey God fully and keep his covenant, as detailed in the Ten Commandments. A key component of these was that the people should remain faithful to the one God, and the fact that they subsequently strayed from their obligations is why they were later punished.

Further on in time, a covenant was made with King David (2 Sam, 7:9–16). This included providing a permanent home for the people of Israel, and that all future monarchs for that nation would stem from David's line.

The final example is revealed by the prophet Jeremiah, as described in 31:31–34. It concerns the promise God made of a New Covenant for the people of Israel and Judah, which some believe applies equally to the whole world. This was that he would put his law: "In their minds and write it on their hearts." Christians believe that this was realized through Jesus, and confirmed by him with his references to: "The cup that seals the covenant" (Mat 26:28; Luk 22:30).

Having already established that people were punished for breaking the covenant and being unfaithful to God, it is appropriate to now review some evidence of how the faithful were rewarded and protected. Starting with the promise made to Abraham as a reward for his righteousness, God tells him that he will, "Bless those who bless you, and whoever curses you I will curse" (Gen 12:3). Shortly after, the Lord tells him not to be afraid because, "I am your shield" (15:1). The prophet is then assured that, even though both he and his wife are beyond the normal age of procreation, they will have a son, Isaac, who will found a great nation. When Isaac was an adult, God confirms that the promise he had made to Abraham would continue through him (26:2–5). Later on, Isaac's own son Jacob was given the same message, and that: "A community of nations will come from you" (35:11–12).

Moses assures the Israelites of God's care and protection during their trek through the wilderness. He says, "For the Lord your God is a merciful God; he will not abandon or destroy you or forget the covenant with your ancestors" (Deut 4:31). Shortly afterwards he added, "Walk in obedience . . . so that you may live long and prosper" (ibid 5:33). Moses thus considers it important to remind the people that the rewards are dependent on them keeping their side of the covenant. The prophet Samuel likewise proclaims that, "The Lord rewards everyone for their righteousness and faithfulness" (1 Sam 26:23).

Unlike his predecessor Saul, King David was rewarded by God for his total obedience, despite his human weaknesses. The Lord asks the prophet Nathan to tell David, "When your days are over and you rest with your ancestors, I will raise up your offspring to succeed you, your own flesh and blood, and I will establish his kingdom" (2 Sam 7:12). This is paralleled in the First Book of Chronicles (17:11), but with "offspring" being replaced with the more specific "sons"; it is also mentioned in several other books including Psalms.

King Asa of Judah was the grandson of Solomon, and he died about 870 BCE. Earlier he had successfully repelled an invasion by the large Cushite army, after declaring his faith in the Lord and calling on him for help (2 Chron 14:11–12). However, on a later occasion he ignored God and instead gave riches to the king of Aram in return for his military intervention. The seer Hanani tells Asa that he has done a foolish thing and, because of this, he would from now on be at war. Later, when the king was ill, he again declined to ask for the Lord's help. Two years later, Asa died (16:7–13). The obvious point being made is that God helps those who ask him for it, but not the ones who ignore him.

David was confident that he would be rewarded in the next life for his faithfulness, in contrast to those who only seek earthly benefits from their actions. He prays, "I shall be vindicated and shall see your face; when I awake I shall be satisfied with seeing your likeness" (Ps 17:15). When David had been helped to avoid being captured by Saul, he sang God's praises announcing that, "'The Lord has rewarded me according to my righteousness" (Ps 18:24). The king makes it clear that there is virtue of maintaining all of God's laws, commands, and decrees when he exclaims, "By them your servant is warned; in keeping them there is great reward" (Ps 19:11).

Another psalm attributed to David also emphasizes that we are rewarded according to our deeds. He states, "Power belongs to you, God, and with you, Lord, is unfailing love; and, you reward everyone according to what they have done" (61:11–12). We do not know who wrote Psalm 91, but Knight[2] states that it appears to be the voice of a temple minister giving assurance to an enquirer that God can and will protect him or her from evil, regardless of its cause. Once this is accepted, a person can confidently say of the Lord, "He is my refuge and my fortress, my God in whom I trust" (v. 2). The psalmist goes on to state that, "No harm will overtake you, no disaster will come near your tent" (v. 10), and continues in the same vein with further examples.

The book of the Hebrew Scriptures with the most references to how God rewards the righteous is Proverbs. The examples relevant to this enquiry concern individual behavior rather than the broader issues of honoring the covenants. Solomon, assuming

2. *The Psalms, Volume 2*, 94–5.

he is the author, says to his son, "Let love and faithfulness never leave you . . . then you will win favor and a good name in the sight of God" (3:3–4). Among the many other proverbs are: "Truly the righteous attain life, but whosoever pursues evil finds death" (11:19), and, "The Lord detests those whose hearts are perverse, but delights in those whose ways are blameless" (11:20). Similar sentiments are expressed in 13:21, "Trouble pursues the sinner, but the righteous are rewarded with good things." And again in 14:14, "The faithless will be fully repaid for their ways, and the good rewarded for theirs."

Another maxim, and one that combines virtuous behavior with eternal recognition, is, "Whoever is kind to the poor lends to the Lord, and he will reward them for what they have done" (19:17). A different virtue is mentioned in 22:4, "Humility is the fear of the Lord; its wages are riches and honor and life." Whilst both the modern and King James versions refer to being humble, the word *sophia* in the Greek LXX translation means wisdom or understanding. Also, although *phobos* can mean fear, it can also have the positive sense of respect, reverence, and awe. Taken together, these changes would inform us that: "wise people are respectful to the Lord, and will be rewarded with riches and honor."

A superficial reading of Proverbs (25:21–22) reveals a rather puzzling message. It states, "If your enemy is hungry, give him food to eat; if he is thirsty, give him water to drink. In doing this, you will heap burning coals on his head, and the Lord will reward you." The reference to burning coals is regarded by most commentators as being a figure of speech for the individual feeling shame, remorse and repentance for his or her evil doings. The unmerited act of kindness forces the transgressor to be conscious of his or her ill-doing. Hopefully, this will result in the pain of regret, along with a resolve to behave better in future. The benevolent individual will be rewarded by God for the good deed, and the proverb appears to be an endorsement of the Commandment to "love your neighbor as yourself."

Finally from Proverbs we have, "A faithful person will be richly blessed, but one eager to get rich will not go unpunished"

(28:20). The GNB translation replaces faithful with honest, whilst the Greek *axiopistos* in the LXX version is rendered worthy but can also mean deserving. Getting rich in this context implies doing so by unscrupulous means; such a person cannot be regarded as faithful and is undeserving of any blessings. By contrast, the one who remains loyal to God and devotes him or herself to hard work will indeed become prosperous, and will find favour with his maker.

Isaiah revealed a whole series of prophesies, and these are grouped under appropriate headings, one of which is "Joy of the redeemed." Although Judah was currently under threat from Syria, this refers to a time in the future when there would be peace, and a descendent of David would be their king. He writes, "Be strong, do not fear; your God will come . . . he will come to save you" (35:4). Another heading is "Comfort for God's people," which includes, "See the Sovereign Lord comes with power . . . see, his reward is with him, and his recompense accompanies him" (40:10). A little further on, the prophet reports God as saying that he promises to help his people, assuring them that, "These are the things I will do; I will not forsake them" (42:16).

The good news for those who remain free from sin continues, with God saying, "For I, the Lord, love justice . . . in my faithfulness I will reward my people and make an everlasting covenant with them" (61:8). This does not refer to a new covenant, but to the one already made with Moses, and also David. God is here stating that, despite this treaty having being broken by the people, he will not abandon his pledge but will renew it. However, it is also a reminder that the Israelites have an obligation to keep their side of the arrangement; they have already suffered greatly for breaking it. God assures those whom he calls "his servants" of salvation, and that, "They will be a people blessed by the Lord, they and their descendents with them" (65:23). This again confirms that the covenant will continue to apply to the generations to come.

Jeremiah conveys the message that, "I the Lord will search the heart and examine the mind, to reward each person according to their conduct, according to what their deeds deserve" (17:10). The message could not be clearer; there is no way of hiding one's true thoughts and behavior from God, and escaping the consequences.

The New Covenant announced by Jeremiah (31:31–33) was mentioned earlier, and Femi Adeyemi[3] regards this as perhaps the highest point of the Scriptures.

Because it includes the statement: "I will put my law in their minds and write it on their hearts" this covenant, unlike the previous ones, is unconditional. It is a promise, with no stipulations on elaborate practices to maintain it from the human side, such as the need for regular animal sacrifices.

Adeyemi discusses the views of several scholars regarding the inclusivity of this covenant. Our behavior, thinking, and feeling would be under the influence of the Holy Spirit, but will this apply only to the Chosen People? The inclusion of the words: "The days are coming" imply a future date, which Christians interpret to mean that the undertaking will be fulfilled with the arrival of the promised Messiah—Jesus (see chapter 14). At the last supper, Jesus said, "The cup is the new covenant in my blood, which is poured out for you" (Luke 22:20). There is support for the view that this is not just a renewal of the Mosaic covenant, but that it is new—a replacement; the old one is now obsolete. Just as God's promise to Abraham that he will bless "all nations" implies inclusivity, so this new covenant likewise applies to every one of God's people.

Jeremiah clearly has confidence that God has the power to, and in fact does, reward his human subjects appropriately. Echoing what he said earlier (7:10), the prophet prays to the Lord, "Your eyes are open to the ways of all mankind; you reward each person according to their conduct and as their deeds deserve" (32:19). By way of confirming what Jeremiah has said, God responds with the comment, "I am the Lord, the God of all mankind. Is anything too hard for me?" (verse 27). What follows is a statement that Judah will fall to the Babylonians because of its sinfulness but, once again, this will not last indefinitely. Verse 37 reports God as saying, "I will bring them back to this place and let them live in safety."

---

3. *What is the new Covenant 'Law' in Jeremiah?*

Quotations from two of the Minor Prophets will suffice to conclude this chapter on rewards for the faithful. Joel reports that, after the suffering Israel had incurred for its sins, God told him that he was now "jealous" for his people, and took pity on them. It was explained in chapter 5 of the present book that the Greek for jealous means zealous or eager, implying keenness to protect. This notion of protectiveness is clearly what God meant when he states, "I will pour out my spirit on all people . . . even on my servants, both men and women, I will pour out my spirit in those days" (Joel 2:28–29). Leslie Allen[4] opines that, superficially, the passage appears to be directed at the nation of Israel as it existed at that time. However, as was the case with Jeremiah's New Covenant (vide supra), it can convincingly be taken to refer to all people, Jews and Gentiles—a Greater Israel.

Amos provides a suitable end to this discussion with a quotation from his vision. Directed at the people of the northern kingdom of Israel, he says, "Seek good, not evil that you may live. Then the Lord God Almighty will be with you, just as you say he is" (5:14). Regardless of time or place, Jew or Gentile, this is surely an appropriate recipe for a good life that will reap its own reward.

In summary, many of the texts that relate to God's rewards are directed at the Israelites as a whole, provided they maintain their covenant obligations. Even when they are punished for their apostasy, the people are ultimately forgiven after a period of suffering. Individuals were also rewarded. The first of these was Abraham who, for his faithfulness and obedience, became a father at a great age, and also the founder of a "great nation." David (in Psalms), Solomon (in Proverbs), Jeremiah, and Amos are among those who state that we are all rewarded according to our deeds. There are plenty of pointers in the Bible to what is required for a good life; we are free to ignore them, but must not then expect to be rewarded for doing so.

---

4. *Joel*, 789.

Chapter 13 ❧

Messianic Prophesies

HINTS PROPHESISING THE COMING of a Messiah, along with some specific details about his future life on earth, occur frequently throughout the Hebrew Scriptures—over 300 have been identified by scholars, although sometimes these include multiple references within the same verse. This is not an insignificant number of citations, and it has led Christians to believe that the passages refer to Jesus, especially as some of the predictions agree closely with details of his life as described in the New Testament. This view is not shared by adherents of the other Abrahamic faiths, whose generally accepted view is that the Messiah, if there is one, is yet to come.

How can we explain this high level of accurate prophesies, written between about 1,500 and 500 years before Christ was born? Accurate, that is, as evidenced by what was subsequently written about him in the New Testament. Some might say the details are so general that they can be made to fit a number of individuals. Others maintain that Jesus intentionally geared his life so as to comply with as many of the predictions as possible.

Another possibility is that many of the New Testament writers compiled their accounts so as to appear to fulfill what they regarded as Old Testament prophesies. However, there remain many who wholly believe that the earlier Scripture passages were genuine prophesies initiated by God, and that Jesus Christ was indeed the promised Messiah. The selection of biblical extracts to be discussed in this chapter may help readers to decide for themselves which of these options they favor.

As has already been mentioned with regard to rewards for the faithful, the earliest references to a future Messiah relate more generally to a special role for Abraham's descendents, for example, "All peoples on earth will be blessed through you" (Gen 12:3). The prophesy of a future ruler being born in the Promised Land is evident from, "The scepter will not depart from Judah . . . until he to whom it belongs shall come and the obedience of the nations shall be his" (49:10). The mention in Numbers (24:17) that, "A star will come out of Jacob; a scepter will rise out of Israel" continues the assertion that Abraham's line will produce a future leader. Does the mention of a star have any link with the star of Bethlehem? Finally from the Pentateuch books, comes another reminder that, "The Lord your God will raise up for you a prophet like me from among you (i.e. the Israelites)" (Deut 18:15).

Whilst many of the Psalms are concerned with praise or prayer, in some cases they appear to reflect what later happened to Jesus. Edward Edinger[1] states that Psalms 2, 22 and 110 are the major Messianic examples; it would be informative to have a look at them here.

The anonymous writer of Psalm 2 starts with a prediction that there will be opposition to the Lord and his anointed one. Nevertheless, the Almighty states that, "I have installed my king on Zion" (and adds) "You are my son; today I have become your father" (verses 7, 8). The final verse (12) exhorts the people to, "Kiss the son, or he will be angry . . . blessed are those who take refuge in him." This reference to "kiss the son" can be interpreted as meaning serve him, fear him, and submit to him.[2] Taken as a whole, all these comments are regarded by some scholars as referring to the future king, Jesus Christ.

Turning now to the second of the Messianic Psalms, Psalm 22, attributed to David, this starts with the last words spoken by Jesus on the cross, "My God, my God, why have you forsaken me?"

1. *The Sacred Psyche*, 58.
2. Wright, *Psalms*, 10.

Verse 7 reflects how he was treated when he was crucified, "All who see me mock me: they hurl insults, shaking their heads." The next verse continues, "'He trusts in the Lord', they say, 'let the Lord rescue him.'" Then verse 18 states, "They divide my clothes among them and cast lots for my garment." The last few verses affirm that all nations will remember the Lord and worship him: "They will proclaim his righteous, declaring to the people yet unborn: He has done it!" (Verse 31). This psalm, and a passage from Isaiah chapter 22 (vide infra), are said to depict the "suffering servant."

Psalm 110, also attributed to David, begins, "The Lord says to my lord: 'Sit at my right hand until I make your enemies a footstool for your feet.'" These opening words, unusual for psalm, suggest that the text describes a revelation made to the author. J. J. Stafford Wright[3] explains that the "lord" (lower case) refers to the Messiah, and that the remainder of the verse prophesizes Jesus' resurrection and ascension, and his ultimate place at the right hand of God. These same words were spoken by Jesus (Mark 12:36).

Verse 4 of the psalm reads, "You are a priest forever, in the order of Melchizedek." Little is known about the king-priest Melchizedek, except that he appeared to Abraham (Gen 14:18), and is regarded as being a timeless, archetypical figure with no beginning and no end. His mention in this psalm is regarded as providing additional emphasis that the Messiah (Jesus) will rule indefinitely, and will have no successor.[4]

There are some other references in Psalms that appear to reflect Jesus' life, other than the three already mentioned. Several are attributed to David and, on the surface, they concern his own life. However, some commentators regard them as prophesising what will happen to Jesus. To quote just a few examples, "The Lord . . . protects his bones, not one of them will be broken" (34:20). Also, "My friends and companions avoid me because of my wounds" (38:11) and, "Even my close friend, someone I trusted . . . has turned against me" (41:9). Finally, there is, "Those who hate me without reason outnumber the hairs on my head" (69:4), "They

3. Ibid., 113.
4. Edinger, *The Sacred Psyche*, 110–7.

put gall in my food and gave me vinegar for my thirst" (ibid 21). These quotations, and many others that have been identified, are repeated or reflected in verses in the New Testament, to which interested readers can refer.

Isaiah contains a number of references that bear a remarkable similarity to episodes in the life of Jesus, starting with his birth. For example, the prophet said, "Therefore the Lord himself will give you a sign: the virgin will conceive and give birth to a son, and will call him Immanuel" (7:14). In chapter 9 there are several verses well-known to Christians, especially in the Advent season: "The people walking in darkness have seen a great light" (9:2) . . . For unto us a child is born, to us a son is given . . . and he will be called Wonderful, Counselor, Mighty God, Everlasting Father, Prince of Peace" (9:6). Further on we read, "A shoot will come up from the stump of Jesse . . . The spirit of the Lord will rest on him" (11:1). Jesse was David's father, so this text is one of many that state that the Messiah will be a descendent of David.

The next Isaiah passage predicts a forerunner, assumed to be John the Baptist: "A voice of one calling: 'In the wilderness prepare the way for the Lord; make straight in the desert a highway for our God'" (40:3). Jesus is often depicted as a good shepherd, and this is suggested by, "See, the Sovereign Lord comes with power . . . He tends his flock like a shepherd: he gathers the lambs in his arms and carries them close to his heart" (40:10–11). That he will come to teach people the ways of God is indicated by, "I am the Lord your God, who teaches you what is best for you, who directs you the way you should go" (48:17). The inclusiveness of Jesus' ministry is predicted by, "I will also make you a light for the Gentiles, that my salvation may reach to the ends of the earth" (49:6).

There are many other passages in Isaiah that are regarded, especially by Christians, as accurately portraying episodes from the life of Jesus, that would only take place some 700 years in the future. This makes it tempting to unpack further examples, but the review of this book will end with just one more reference. Along with Psalm 22 (vide supra), verses in Isaiah chapters 52 and 53 are regarded as depicting Jesus as the "suffering servant." Chapter

52:14 reads, "Just as there were many who were appalled at him—his appearance was so disfigured beyond that of any human being." In the following chapter it states, "But he was pierced for our transgressions, he was crushed for our iniquities . . . by his wounds we are healed. We all, like sheep, have gone astray" (verses 5–6).

The predictions of the prophet Jeremiah which reiterate that a Messiah would be born of David's line, and that a New Covenant will be put into the hearts and minds of all people, has already been mentioned in the previous chapter. There is also reference to David in Ezekiel (34:23–14), namely, "I will place over them one shepherd, my servant David, and he will tend them and be their shepherd." However, commentators usually interpret this as meaning the "seed" of David, or a ruler with the "exemplary attributes" of David.[5] Whilst Daniel's apocalyptic vision is often described in figurative terms, his image in chapter 7, verses 13–14, is pertinent. He writes, "I looked, and there before me was one like a son of man, coming with the clouds of heaven . . . He was given authority, glory and sovereign power; all nations and peoples of every language worshiped him. His dominion is an everlasting dominion that will not pass away."

Another accurate prophesy, this time of the place where the Messiah will be born, is found in Micah (5:2). It reads, "But you, Bethlehem Ephrathah, though you are small among the clans of Judah, out of you will come for me one who will be ruler over Israel." There is some uncertainty about the inclusion of the word Ephrathah in this statement. It can mean fruitful but also worthless, or refer to a geographical district. Alternatively, it could indicate the founder of the town, as indicated for example, in 1 Chronicles (4:4), "These are the descendents of Hur, the firstborn of Ephrathah and father of Bethlehem.

A rather cryptic statement is made by God to the minor prophet Haggai (2:7). It reads, "I will shake all the nations, and what is desired by all nations will come, and I will fill this house with glory." John James[6] reports that many commentators interpret that the "desire" was for a Messiah, and that this was fulfilled

5. McGregor, *Ezekiel*, 739.
6. *Haggai, Zechariah and Malachi*, 34.

with the coming of Jesus. Another somewhat indirect statement is made by Habakkuk (2:14), which has a close parallel in Isaiah (11:9): "For the earth will be filled with the glory of the Lord, as the waters cover the sea." Is this also a prophesy of Christ's coming, as savior of the whole world?

A more obvious foretelling is found in Zechariah (9:9), "See, your king comes to you, righteous and victorious, lowly and riding on a donkey, on a colt, the foal of a donkey." The New Testament reports that this is just how Jesus entered Jerusalem (Matt 21:5–6). Chapter 11 tells how God spoke to Zechariah, telling him to: "Shepherd the flock marked for slaughter" (verse 1), and continues with the same theme until the prophet resigns in frustration. Zechariah then says, "If you think it best, give me my pay; but if not, keep it. So they paid me thirty pieces of silver" (11:12). John James[7] explains that the story is an allegory. Israel is the "flock," and their leaders are bad shepherds. The prophet is asked to take the role of God's own good shepherd, but he rejects the idea. This is held to be predictive of the future rejection of Jesus. Added to this, is it beyond credibility to equate the reference to thirty pieces of silver with what Judas was paid for betraying Jesus?

Zechariah has more to say. The Lord prophesizes to him, "They will look on me, the one they have pierced, and they will mourn for him as one mourns for an only child" (12:10). The "piercing" is believed by some to refer to the crucifixion of Jesus (as was Isaiah 52:14, vide supra) and, likewise, "Strike the shepherd, and the sheep will be scattered" (13:7) to Christ as shepherd, and the subsequent dispersion of his disciples.

Finally, the last book of the Scriptures, Malachi, expands the message previously delivered by Isaiah (40:10–11), that is usually regarded as referring to John the Baptist. Malachi reports God as telling him, "I will send my messenger, who will prepare the way for me. Then suddenly the Lord you are seeking will come to his temple; the messenger of the covenant, whom you desire, will come" (3:1). James[8] explains that two messengers are mentioned here. The first

7. Ibid., 123–6.
8. Ibid., 156–7.

is held to be John the Baptist, whilst the second—the messenger of the covenant—is Jesus himself, who was to visit the temple on many occasions, the first time as a child aged 12 (Luke, 2:27).

In the quest to find out what we can learn about God from the Hebrew Scriptures, the present chapter offered passages that many believe provides evidence to suggest that the Lord intended to send a representative to earth—the Messiah. Over a period of about 1,000 years, he kept giving clues about this in his messages to the prophets. Whilst not all religions acknowledge that Jesus was indeed the promised one, it is remarkable that there are sufficient references that can be linked to him, to enable Christians to conclude that this was the case.

Some texts are more general, just stating that an anointed one, king, savior, or leader will be born sometime in the future. Various ancestors are mentioned, starting with Abraham, and including David and Jesse. Two New Testament passages provide Jesus' genealogy: Matthew (1:1–17) and Luke (3:23–38). Whilst they are not in full agreement, they both include these three ancestors. The expectation that a Messiah will come to redeem the nation and the church, has provided inspiration throughout Israel's history, and still does to the Jewish people today.

The predictions become more interesting when they start to be more specific. In combination, they state that he will be preceded by a messenger from the wilderness (John the Baptist). He will be born in Bethlehem, and his mother will be a virgin. The mention of a star in Numbers (24:17) may be relevant. The Messiah will ride on a donkey. There will be opposition, and he will be betrayed, with his betrayer receiving 30 pieces of silver. He will be mocked, insulted, pierced (crucified), and given gall and vinegar to drink. His clothes will be divided among others by lot. His last words on the cross will be, "My God, my God, why have you forsaken me?" The Messiah will come for all the nations.

Are all these details that are reflected in the life of Jesus, many years later, just coincidences? Opinion is divided so you, the reader, will have to decide for yourself.

Chapter 14 ✑

God Answers Prayers

WHY DO PEOPLE PRAY? To a non-believer, talking to somebody who is not there, whether silently or audibly, may seem a futile thing to do. The pious will respond that there *is* somebody there—God is everywhere, including in our minds, so he can hear our prayers. A devil's advocate may then say that, if there is a God, and he hears the prayers, why does he not respond to them? The questioner may then continue: why are there still wars, why is there so much evil in the world, and why are there so many incurable diseases?

These questions are justified, and are not easy to address. They fall into the big issue of whether we have freedom to act, or whether God controls all our actions. A full debate on this question is beyond the scope of this book. A believer may, however, wish to summarise his or her standpoint by saying that you cannot have it both ways; either we are free to act as we wish (within the confines of the law), or all our actions are controlled. Whilst the latter may at least ensure a peaceful world, human beings would be under the control of a higher power at all times, with no independence.

Whether or not the story of Adam and Eve is literally true, or is an allegory, the message is that the couple in the garden had the freedom to disobey God's command not to eat the forbidden fruit, and they ate some (Gen 2:17; 3:6). The ability to act contrary to what God would like us to do remains with human beings to this day. It may sadden God to witness this but, those who are parents can only try and pass on appropriate moral guidance to their children, and then leave them to make their own decisions in life.

What do people pray about? There are many topics, including praising God and thanking him for good things; asking for help for other individuals, especially those who are sick; praying that there will be peace in the world; asking for forgiveness for one's own sins or those of others; seeking guidance about decisions that need to be made; requesting help to overcome one's own sickness or other difficulty. There is no limit to the issues that can be raised, or the time spent in prayer. Different religions have their own rituals and practices. For Christians, there is much advice on prayer given in the New Testament, including a useful example—The Lord's Prayer—that is routinely included in church services (Matt 6:9–13).

Harold Koenig[1] (2001; 2002) conducted several research studies on the role that religion can play in the lives of individuals. Among his findings is that religious beliefs may provide people with a form of control over health matters that their non-religious peers do not have. In particular, when people pray to God, believing that he is capable of intervening, they are actually doing something to help improve their situation. Remarkably, Koenig also found that religious activities might even be associated with longer survival of up to seven years.

Other researchers have also found indications of a link between religion and aspects of health, but should all this be attributed to, at best, faith healing or, at worst, self-delusion? As with the freedom versus determinism dilemma, there is no easy answer. Nevertheless, many people remain convinced that their prayers have been answered not just once, but many times over. They may say that just one example could be a coincidence, and perhaps also two. However, the situation changes as the number of examples increases. This then becomes what Peter Donovan[2] calls the "cumulative case." He concluded from his own research on religious

1. *The Healing Power of Faith* (2001); *A Commentary* (2002), 20–3.
2. *Interpreting Religious Experiences.*

117

experiences, that the sheer weight of evidence of many incidences can be regarded as drawing progressively closer to an acceptable proof. As with other issues raised, it is for each individual to come to his or her own view on this matter.

It is clear, from the number of scriptural references to people praying to God, that there was confidence that the prayers would be heard, and that they would be answered. As was already mentioned in chapter 9 (healing), Genesis reports that, in an attempt to help Abimelek with his barrenness, "Abraham prayed to God, and God healed Abimelek" (20:17). When the prophet's servant needed water for his camels and himself, he asked the Almighty, "Lord, God of my master Abraham, make me successful today" (24:12). His prayer was successful. A little later on, Abraham's son likewise asked for help: "Isaac prayed to the Lord on behalf of his wife." His need was for her to bear children, and again this was granted (25:21).

Sometimes the texts refer to this as "talking to God," rather than prayer as such. Exodus (3:13–14) states that Moses said to the Lord, "Suppose I go to the Israelites and say to them, 'the God of your fathers has sent me to you.'" He then follows with a question concerning the Lord's name, and is told to answer, "I am who I am" (see also this book, chapter 5). During their journey to the Promised Land, the Israelites often complained about their hardships, and God was so angered that he sent fire to the camp. Moses was asked to intervene: "He prayed to the Lord and the fire died down" (Num 11:2).

Many of the people then started to die from snake bite, but they acknowledged that this was punishment for their sins. They asked Moses to pray for help, and the Lord replied, "Make a snake and put it on a pole; anyone who is bitten can look at it and live" (Num 21:7). Moses made a snake out of bronze, and it served its purpose. Although this is not the generally accepted origin of the medical symbol of a serpent twisted around a staff, perhaps it could have been an early influence, based on this association between snakes and healing.

Moses makes a general statement about prayer, as recorded in Deuteronomy (4:7): "What other nation is so great as to have their gods near them the way the Lord our God is whenever we pray to him." The implication is that, not only are the prayers heard, but they are answered by actual deeds. A clear example of this is related in Judges (16:28): "Then Samson prayed to the Lord, 'Please God, strengthen me just once more, and let me with one blow get revenge on the Philistines for my two eyes.'" This well-known story continues by describing how Samson mustered sufficient strength to bring down the temple, killing his enemies but sadly also himself.

Another example concerns the prophet Samuel, who was himself conceived after his mother Hannah prayed for a son (1 Sam, 1:11). Near the end of his life, he told the people he was going to convince them of the superiority of his God, by asking him for unseasonably severe weather. The narrative states: "Then Samuel called the Lord, and that same day the Lord sent thunder and rain" (12:18). The Second Book of Samuel reports many examples of David talking to God. The final one tells of a plague inflicted on the people of Israel, because he had taken a census without God's authorization. David tries to make amends for his sins: "Then the Lord answered his prayer, and the plague on Israel was stopped" (24:25).

The prophet Elijah used prayer to demonstrate to the pagans the pre-eminence of his God over Baal. He prayed, "Answer me, Lord, answer me, so these people will know that you, Lord, are God, and that you are turning their hearts back again" (1 Kgs 18:36). The Almighty responded by sending down fire to burn up a sacrifice, and this convinced the apostates. Some time later Elijah feared for his life, and ran into the wilderness. Overcome with fatigue and hunger, he sat down under a broom bush, "And prayed that he might die. 'I have had enough, Lord,' he said. 'Take my life'" (ibid 19:4). In response, God sent an angel who gave him food and drink. This strengthened him, and he continued his journey.

When Elisha and his servant were surrounded by the Aramean army, the prophet knew there were forces that would protect them, but the servant could not see them. Elisha then prayed, "Open his eyes, Lord, so that he may see" (2 Kgs 6:17–18). God did so, and the servant then saw their own troops. As the enemy charged toward them, the prophet again prayed saying, "Strike this army with blindness," and this was immediately done. When the Aramean forces had been lured into the city of Samaria, and were at the mercy of the defending army, Elisha prayed yet again, this time requesting that the enemy's eyes be opened; this was then granted (22–23). The prophet then exercised compassion and had the Arameans given refreshment and sent away. This resulted in a cessation of any more hostilities by them.

Solomon offered a prayer of dedication for the temple: "Now, my God, may your eyes be open and your ears attentive to the prayers offered in this place" (2 Chron 6:40). When he had finished, "Fire came down from heaven and consumed the burnt offering and the sacrifices, and the glory of the Lord filled the temple" (7:1). The same book reports that Hezekiah prayed for people who had not purified themselves in the prescribed way, before joining in the Passover feast. He asks, "May the Lord, who is good, pardon everyone who sets their heart on seeking God—the Lord . . . even if they are not clean according to the rules of the sanctuary. The Lord heard Hezekiah and healed the people" (30:19–20).

After hearing about the destruction of Jerusalem, the prophet Nehemiah relates how he prayed to God. He admitted that the people of Israel had sinned, and asked, "Lord, let your ear be attentive to the prayer of your servants who delight in revering your name" (1:11). Nehemiah then travelled to Jerusalem, where he encouraged the rebuilding of the city wall. At each stage of the work there was opposition, and the threat of trouble. The prophet again addressed the Lord saying, "We prayed to our God and posted a guard day and night to meet this threat" (4:9). Despite further challenges, the task was completed and worship rituals resumed.

Many Psalms read as if they are being addressed directly to God, either as praise, lamentation, or pleas for help. Specific phrases indicate that the writer (often allegedly David) is praying out loud. Examples include: "Answer me when I call to you, my righteous God" (4:1), and "Hear my cry for help, my King and my God, for to you I pray" (5:2). Psalm 6:9 indicates that the request had been heard: "The Lord has heard my cry for mercy; the Lord accepts my prayer." That it has been suitably actioned is implied by what follows: "All my enemies will be overwhelmed with shame and anguish" (6:10).

Another earnest request from David is found in Psalm 17:1, namely, "Hear me, Lord, my plea is just; listen to my cry. Hear my prayer—it does not arise from deceitful lips." Likewise, "Listen to my prayer, O God, do not ignore my plea; hear me and answer me" (55:1). Here, as in many others, David is asking that the Lord will control, or punish, his enemies. That he is confident his prayers will be acted upon is evidenced by, "Praise awaits you, our God, in Zion; to you our vows will be fulfilled. You who answer prayer, to you all people will come" (65:1–2). In similar vein: "Praise be to God, who has not rejected my prayer or withheld his love from me" (66:20).

The writer of Proverbs has two comments about prayer in the same chapter. Firstly, he states, "The Lord detests the sacrifice of the wicked, but the prayer of the upright pleases him" (15:8). He reiterates this in a similar message, "The Lord is far from the wicked, but he hears the prayers of the righteous" (verse 29).

Isaiah has something to say on most topics, and prayer is no exception. Jerusalem was being threatened by the Assyrian army, but King Hezekiah had put false hopes in a treaty with Egypt to protect him. When the enemy tried to encourage the Judeans to surrender, the king sent a message to Isaiah asking him to seek God's help: "Therefore pray for the remnant that still survives" (37:4). Presumably the prophet did as he was asked. In a reference to the Assyrian commander's exhortation to capitulate, he duly reports, "This is what the Lord says: do not be afraid of what you have heard." The message continues: "Listen, when he hears a certain report, I will make him want to return to his own country, and there I will have him cut down with the sword" (verses 6–7).

The next step of the story occurs when Hezekiah, who is acknowledged to have been a good king, received a message from his

Assyrian counterpart, ridiculing the Lord. He decides to offer his own prayer: "And Hezekiah prayed to the Lord . . . you alone are the God over all the kingdoms of the earth . . . now, Lord our God, deliver us from his hand" (verses 16–20). Isaiah receives a long reply on behalf of the king, ending with, "I will defend this city and save it, for my sake and for the sake of David my servant" (verse 35). Incredibly, the narrative then reports that 185,000 Assyrian troops were put to death in their camp by "an angel of the Lord." Although Jerusalem escaped invasion this time, the Babylonians did succeed in conquering the city about 130 years later.

A further citation from Isaiah reports God as saying that there is an appropriate place where prayers can be offered—presumably the temple. He writes that, for those who are faithful to him, "These I will bring to my holy mountain and give them joy in my house of prayer . . . for my house will be called a house of prayer for all nations" (56:7). Here again we have the notion of inclusiveness; foreigners are treated according to their attitude, not their birth.[3]

Jeremiah reported on an unusual case of God asking the prophet *not* to pray. This was when the Judeans were to be punished for their idolatry. God says, "So do not pray for this people nor offer any plea or petition for them: do not plead with me, for I will not listen to you" (7:16). The nation, along with Jerusalem, was conquered by the Babylonians, and many of its citizens were deported. Later, Jeremiah writes to the Judean exiles, quoting what God had subsequently told him: "Seek the peace and prosperity of the city to which I have carried you into exile. Pray to the Lord for it" (29:7). God then promised to bring them back to their homeland after 70 years, and comments through Jeremiah, "Then you will call on me and come and pray to me, and I will listen to you" (verse 12).

Another example of Jeremiah praying, and receiving a response, concerns a small band of Judeans during the time of the exile. They approached the prophet and asked him, "Please hear our petition and pray to the Lord your God for this entire remnant

3. Kidner, *Isaiah*, 665.

... pray that (he) will tell us where to go and what we should do" (42:2–3). Instead of an instant response, the text states that it was 10 days later that Jeremiah received an answer. It said that the group should stay in Judah and God would help them; if they went to Egypt they would suffer disaster. However, the group did not believe that the prophet was telling the truth, and they did go to Egypt, taking some of the other Judeans with them. Some years later, Egypt was itself invaded by the Babylonians.

The reason why Daniel was thrown into the lion's den was because he defied instructions to only pray to the king. The text describes how, "Three times a day he got down on his knees and prayed, giving thanks to his God, just as he had done before" (Dan 6:10). In due course, Daniel learned from the Scriptures that the destruction of Jerusalem would last 70 years. He "Prayed to the Lord my God and confessed . . . " (9:4), admitting that the people had sinned, but asking that mercy be shown and that forgiveness would come quickly.

A response to the prayer was received almost immediately. It took the form of a visit from the angel Gabriel, who explained that it would take multiples of "sevens" (years) before the sin was atoned for (20–27). Scholars are divided on how this is resolved, but one view is that it can compute to 490 years, and may be a prediction linked to the coming of Jesus Christ.[4]

The final example of prayer to be discussed is taken from the minor prophet Habakkuk. This entire, short text is a dialogue with God, starting with questions concerning why wickedness can go unpunished, and why the oppressors from Babylon have not themselves suffered a fate worse than did the Chosen People. God's reply is that justice will be done in its own good time. Chapter 3 begins, "A prayer of Habakkuk the prophet . . . Lord, I have heard of your fame; I stand in awe of your deeds, Lord." This continues for all the 19 remaining verses, and contains indications that it is in the form of a psalm to be sung. The prophet acknowledges God's deeds for his people in the past, and expresses confidence that his covenant will be maintained.

4. Ferguson, *Daniel*, 759.

What conclusions can be drawn from the evidence that so many writers made references to prayer? Were they all deluded in thinking that speaking to someone up there, either audibly or silently, would result in their words being not only heard, but acted upon? The accounts include reports on how enemies were defeated, and the Israelites protected. Also that fire descended on sacrifices on more than one occasion, blindness was inflicted and then lifted, and that Samson was given the strength to demolish the temple.

Can we regard the inclusion of examples where the requests appear to have been answered as just coincidences, with those that were ignored being conveniently omitted from the biblical accounts? The faithful believe that God *does* hear their prayers, and *does* respond, although not always in the way they might expect or wish for. Once again it remains for each individual to decide for themself, provided he or she has tried it first.

Chapter 15 ❧

So What *Do* Know about God?

THE SIMPLE ANSWER TO the question posed by the chapter heading is: a surprisingly large amount! The list of attributes and characteristics identified by the present writer is by no means exhaustive, and readers may wish to add some items of their own. But what does it mean to *know* somebody? If we know them well, this will include aspects such as someone we can trust, and be relied upon to help when needed. It will be a person who is prepared to listen to us; respond to our requests; is always available when needed; who cares about us; who guides us. Maybe it is someone who can even anticipate our needs and then smoothes the path before us. Above all, it will be somebody who is a friend. Is this now starting to sound rather like the way the faithful might talk about their God?

This enquiry commenced with an investigation into the early signs of a belief in a supernatural power, and was followed by a review of the origins and beliefs of the world's major religions. Evidence was then drawn from the Hebrew Scriptures (Old Testament), which are accepted as authoritative by adherents of the Jewish, Christian and Islamic faiths. It was pointed out that, although none of the original manuscripts have yet been found, by drawing on legal criteria the books can be regarded as providing reliable evidence. It is, however, necessary to take account of textural errors that could have occurred during the many stages of copying, editing, and translation that have led to the versions we read today. In addition, the social, political and cultural situation that existed at the time of writing has to be considered when trying to interpret the writer's intended meaning (the SIL).

The main objective of the study was to see what the Scriptures could reveal about the nature of the Abrahamic God, his attributes, and what he does. The challenge with this task was not so much trying to find relevant material, but in how to select and summarise from the wealth of evidence available. It may be helpful to review what has been discovered so far, before bringing the investigation to a close with a conclusion, and a mention of some final attributes.

The obvious place to start the quest was right at the beginning, and to ponder how belief in a power greater than human beings could have originated. It may have been that our ancestors needed a way of accounting for phenomena that could not be explained with the scientific knowledge of the time. Another influence could have been the need to try and ensure that the annual cycle of animal breeding and crop growing continued, by venerating some unseen deity that was believed to control nature. Chapter 1 mentioned that the earliest burial practices date from about 100,000 years ago, and that at least one artifact that may have represented a god probably dates back some 30,000 years. Excavations have uncovered what could be a temple site that is 12,000 years old.

It did not take long after this for various pagan deities to be conceived, along with the rituals and priestly casts needed to keep in favor with them, such as those in ancient Egypt. The earliest major world religions are believed to have started in the third millennium BCE. Judaism, Christianity and Islam each acknowledge that their beginnings stem from God's call to Abraham in about 2,000 BCE. This is related in the book of Genesis, acknowledged by many to have been written by Moses, and draws on earlier oral traditions. A novel idea that has been voiced is that God was a visitor from another world. Whilst this is a distinctly minority view, there are some intriguing texts that refer to smoke, fire and noise resembling a rocket ship. Chapter 5 also discussed the question of what is God's name.

The enquiry then moved on to the qualities that can be ascribed to the Almighty, as revealed in the Hebrew Scriptures, in addition to the often mentioned omnipotent, omniscient, and omnipresent. That he is described as unique, holy, majestic, powerful, merciful and loving is by no means the complete list. Several chapters discussed evidence relating to the things that God does, starting appropriately with the act of creating the universe and our world in it. It is doubtful that science will ever be able to explain what was there right at the beginning, before time began. Even Einstein's $E=MC^2$ equation only suggests the possibility of it being pure energy. Is it possible to improve on the biblical statement that, "In the beginning was God"?

Two chapters examined the topic of miracles. Does God change the laws of nature in order to perform miracles, or does he use them at the appropriate time and place, in order to intervene? People in ancient times did not have the knowledge of science that we have today to help them explain seemingly miraculous events. Possible explanations were suggested for the act of creation, the flood, the destruction of Sodom and Gomorrah, Lot's wife turning to salt, the parting of the Red Sea, and other incidents.

Many of the healing miracles can be understood using our present medical knowledge. Abimelek was no doubt solely responsible for his harem's inability to conceive, and the cause may have been psychosomatic. It could have respond to measures ranging from a change of diet to what we would today call psychotherapy.

There are 613 laws cited in the Pentateuch, although it is not always clear how many Moses might have created himself as expansions of the original Decalogue. He needed to try and maintain unity and faithfulness among the Israelites during their wanderings and early settlement. Many laws relate to sacrificial requirements, and some are cruel to animals. Capital punishment was prescribed for transgressions that would seem relatively minor today.

Linked to the laws are God's involvement in judging and punishing, and he was widely acknowledged as the ultimate arbitrator. Whilst some of the punishments were meted out to individuals, the nations of Israel and Judah both suffered for their respective apostasies by being overrun by their enemies, despite being warned. It does seem harsh that Moses was not allowed to enter the Promised Land because of a single transgression, despite his immense service to God and the Hebrew nation. However, the Lord also rewards those who remain faithful in terms of the Covenant. He even kept his promise to restore the land of the Chosen People, after they had endured a period of exile. God also continued to remind people of his pledge to build a great nation from the descendents of Abraham.

Following on from this are the prophesies concerning the coming of a Messiah from David's line. Some believe he is still to come, whilst Christians maintain that the Messiah came in the personhood of Jesus Christ. Indeed, the Scriptures contain some remarkably accurate predictions of Jesus' life, including the virgin birth, Bethlehem, riding a donkey, persecution, and being pierced (crucified). However, some may say that either the texts were edited to agree with what happened, or that Jesus intentionally manipulated aspects of his life to comply with such predictions.

The final example of what God does concerned answering prayers. On the face of it, addressing someone who is not physically present and asking for help, seems a strange thing to do, and even more so when it is done silently. Nevertheless, there are many references in the Scriptures to prayer and examples of them being answered. If this occurs often enough, the weight of evidence indicates that this is more than a series of coincidences. Modern research shows that those who pray feel that they are doing something to help a situation, and thus have more control over their lives than have those who do not subscribe to the power of prayer.

From the information contained in the preceding chapters, it is clear that we can learn a great deal about the Abrahamic God from the Hebrew Scriptures. Through this knowledge, the Lord ceases to be just a remote entity acknowledged by the faithful, and instead becomes a being with characteristics and a personality. When we feel that we can anticipate the likes, dislikes, and responses of an individual, we can grow to know and trust him or her. This makes the whole prospect of a personal God more feasible. As Jeremiah (9:24) states, quoting what God had said to him, "But let the one who boasts boast about this: that they have the understanding to know me, that I am the Lord." For Christians, there is much more to learn about him from the New Testament, but that is beyond of the intended scope of the present book.

Before bringing this enquiry to a close, there are just three more indications to be mentioned that may help to inform on the nature of God. The first concerns God's voice. Whilst there are many comments in the Scriptures that include: "Declares the Lord" (Jer 51:39), "The Lord said to me" (Deut 2:31), "The word of the Lord came to me" (Ezek 7:1), or similar, these are usually followed by reported speech. Job (33:14–16) mentions the ways that the Lord can communicate with us: "For God does speak—now one way, now another—though no one perceives it. In a dream, in a vision of the night, when deep sleep falls on people as they slumber in their beds, he may speak in their ears and terrify them with warnings." More interesting, perhaps, are the reports of God's audible, direct speech.

Specific references to this include the story of Samuel's call, as related in his first book, chapter 3. Verse 4 reads, "Then the Lord called to Samuel. Samuel answered 'Here I am.'" The call is repeated (verse 6) and again in verse 10. Verse 11 commences: "And the Lord said to Samuel . . . ," and continues with further verbatim statements. Isaiah's call is similar, when the prophet reports, "Then I heard the voice of the Lord saying, 'Whom shall I send?'" (Isa 6:8). Further dialogue then follows.

Whilst these examples clearly imply that God's voice was actually heard, in each case this was by just a single person, with no other witnesses to confirm it. There are, however, a few cases of the sound being witnessed by several people at the same time. When Moses was involved with receiving the Decalogue on Mount Sinai, the narrative states that there was a loud trumpet blast, the mountain trembled and was covered in smoke, and the Lord descended in fire. Exodus (19:19) reads, "As the sound of the trumpet grew louder and louder, Moses spoke and the voice of God answered him." Although the passage confirms what the Lord said to Moses, and presumably Aaron who was with him, on this occasion it does not say that the rest of the Israelites heard specific words.

Related in the format of a song, and employing rather picturesque language, David mentions a similar experience to that of Moses. Samuel's second book, chapter 22, relates how David called to the Lord, and then, "The earth trembled and quaked . . . smoke rose from his nostrils . . . The Lord thundered from heaven; the voice of Most High resounded" (verses 8–14). Again, no actual words of God are mentioned.

A novel twist occurs in another story involving the Lord's presence and extreme elements. God tells Elijah to stand on a mountain whilst he passes by. 1 Kings (19: 11–13) states that, "A great and powerful wind tore the mountain apart . . . but the Lord was not in the wind." Then there was an earthquake, but he was not there either. This was followed by a fire, but still the Lord was absent. The story continues, "And after the fire came a gentle whisper"; this *was* the voice of God.

The declared intention throughout this book has been to confine the evidence to that revealed in the Hebrew Scriptures. However, this discussion would be incomplete without the inclusion of two passages from the New Testament, as they are the most explicit biblical examples of the audible voice of God being heard simultaneously by groups of people. As with the earlier examples, they too mention phenomena associated with the elements. The first concerns the baptism of Jesus. Mark (1:10–11) states, "Just as Jesus was coming out of the water, he saw the heaven being torn open and the Spirit descending on him like a dove. And a voice came from heaven: 'You are my Son, whom I love; with you I am well pleased.'"

This story is paralleled in Luke (3:21). In the second example, Matthew records how Jesus took some of his disciples onto a high mountain, and Moses and Elijah appeared. Then, "A bright cloud came down and covered them, and a voice from the cloud said,

'This is my son, whom I love; with him I am well pleased. Listen to him!'" (17:5).

So, not only does God have attributes and perform actions, he also has a voice that can be heard, not only silently, or by putting thoughts into our minds, but as an audible sound that can be witnessed simultaneously by many people. However, has anybody actually *seen* God? Although in the New Testament, John (1:18) states, "No one has ever seen God," some Scripture passages seem to suggest that this is not true.

Genesis (3:8) reports that, "The man and his wife heard the sound of the Lord God as he was walking in the garden," but it does not state that they actually saw him. Later on, Jacob says of a place he had just named 'Peniel,' "It is because I saw God face to face, yet my life was spared" (Gen 32:30). Although this may be so, when he had asked the man to whom he was referring for his name, he received no answer.

Three passages in Exodus seem to suggest a visual sighting of God. In the first, "Moses and Aaron, Nadab and Abihu, and seventy elders of Israel went up and saw the God of Israel" (24:9–10). Whilst this appears to be a significant reference, it is puzzling that the passage does not include any description of the Godhead except a mention of his feet. According to Exodus (33:11), "The Lord would speak to Moses face to face." However, this is ambiguous, as it does not specifically say they *saw* face to face. A similar version of this occurs in Numbers (12:8).

Another Exodus passage relates how Moses asked to see God's glory, but the Lord replied, "You cannot see my face, for no one may see me and live" (33:20), which appears to vindicate John's statement (vide supra). Nevertheless, the prophet was permitted to see the back of God after he had walked by. In the book of Isaiah, the prophet states, "In the year that King Uzziah dies, I saw the Lord, high and exalted, seated on a throne" (6:1)? Does this mean that he did actually look upon the face of God, or was it some sort of manifestation?

Unfortunately, we are no closer to learning what God looks like from these passages. As God the Holy Spirit, in any event we would not expect him to have a permanent form, but to be able to manifest himself anywhere, any time, and in any form that he wishes.

It is perhaps appropriate that the last topic to be discussed in this book concerns the promise of a life hereafter. Whilst the New Testament abounds with references to this, it is also not neglected in its Hebrew Scripture counterpart. Genesis (5:24) states that, "Enoch walked faithfully with God, then he was no more, because God took him away." Whilst this may be open to different interpretations, what God said to Abraham is unambiguous: "You, however, will go to your ancestors in peace and be buried at a good old age" (Gen 15:15). The prophet's relatives may be far away, but the immortality of the soul will be united with them after his bodily death.

The statement included in Hannah's prayer is likewise quite specific: "The Lord brings death and makes alive; he brings down to the grave and raises up" (1 Sam 2:6). It is reported in 1 Kings (2:11) that, "Elijah went up to heaven in a whirlwind." This passage was also cited in chapter 5 of the present book, as an example of what seems like modern space rocket activity. Job is convinced that one day, when his "Skin has been destroyed," he "Will see God; I myself will see him with my own eyes" (19:26–27). In similar vein, David proclaims, "I shall be vindicated and see your face; when I awake, I shall be satisfied with seeing your likeness" (Ps 17:15).

The writer of Ecclesiastes initially questions whether or not we are eventually united with God, "Who knows if the human spirit rises upwards and if the spirit of the animal goes down into the earth?" (3:21). Later, he seems more certain: "And the dust returns to the ground it came from, and the spirit returns to God who gave it" (12:7). Isaiah is also sure of the afterlife: "But your dead will live, Lord; their bodies will rise—let those who dwell in the dust wake up and shout for joy" (26:19). Finally, Daniel writes of his vision of the end times, stating that the names of those who are worthy are written in a book, and (only) those people will be "delivered." Then, "Multitudes who sleep in the dust of the earth will awake: some to everlasting life, others to shame and contempt" (12:2).

We have finally come to the end of our quest to find out we can about the God of Abraham, as contained in the Scriptures. Instead of him being regarded as just some nebulous entity, hopefully we can now recognize qualities in him to which we can relate and understand. Not only that, but he is someone who freely chooses to enter into a relationship with the human beings he has created. This is not to try and anthropomorphize the Almighty, as he remains omnipotent, omniscient and omnipresent, but it is surely more comfortable to feel that we are in touch with a God we now know a little better.

Bibliography

Adeyemi, Femi. "What is the new Covenant 'Law' in Jeremiah 31:33?" *Bibliotheca Sacra* 163 (2002) 312–23.

Allen, Leslie C. "Joel." In *New Bible Commentary*, edited by D. A. Carson et al., 780–91. Nottingham, UK: IVP, 2011.

Anonymous. *Gobeklitepe, the Oldest Temple in the World*. (Accessed August, 2016). http://gobeklitepe.info.

Anonymous. *Religion Facts*. (August, 2016). www.religionfacts.com.

Anonymous. *The Design of the Old Testament*. (Accessed September, 2016). www.askelm.com/restoring/res006.htm.

Anonymous. *Islam: the True Religion of God Almighty*. (Accessed April, 2016). www.answering-christianity.com/allah1.htm.

Anonymous. 10 *Plagues Explained Scientifically*. (November, 2014). http://imgur.com/gallery/x97eY.

Anonymous. *All 613 Commandments in the Old Testament Law*. (2010). http://gods-word-first.org/bible-study/613commandments.html

Anonymous. "Studies in Theology and Hume's 'Essays on Miracles.'" *Bibliotheca Sacra* 71 (1914) 105–31.

Arnold, B. T. "Recent trends in the study of Jeremiah." *Ashland Theological Journal*, 25 (1993) 76–83.

Barber, Michael, John Bergsma, Brant Pitre, and John Kincaid, John. "What did Jesus Sing at the Last Supper?" (April, 2009). *The Sacred Page*. http://www.thesacredpage.com/2009/04/what-did-jesus-sing-at-last-supper.html.

Baker, David, W. "Habakkuk." In *New Bible Commentary*, edited by D. A. Carson, R. T. France, J. A. Motyer, & G. J. Wenham, 840–7. Nottingham, UK: IVP, 2011.

Basham, A. L. "Hinduism." In *The Concise Encyclopaedia of Living Faiths, edited by* R. C. Zaehner, 217–55). London: Hutchinson, 1971.

Biddle, M. E. *Deuteronomy, Smyth and Helwys Bible Commentary*. Macon: Smyth & Helwys, 2003.

Bimson, John J. "1 and 2 Kings." In *New Bible Commentary*, edited by D. A. Carson et al., 334–87. Nottingham, UK: IVP, 2011.

Butler, Trent C. *Holman Concise Bible Dictionary*. Nashville, Ten: Holman Reference, 2011.

Butt, Kyle. *Egyptian Magicians, Snakes, and Rods*. (2005). http://apologeticspress. org/apcontent.aspx?category=11&article=1704.

Clines, David J. A. "Job." In *New Bible Commentary*, edited by D. A. Carson et al., 459–84. Nottingham, UK: IVP, 2011.

Crabtree, Vexen. *A List of All Religions and Belief Systems*. (2013). http://www. humanreligions.info/religions.html.

Dawkins, Richard (2006). *The God Delusion*. Boston NY: Houghton Miffin.

Dockery, D. S. "The History of Pre-critical Biblical Interpretations." *Faith and Mission*, 10 (1992) 1–30.

Donovan, Peter. *Interpreting Religious Experience*. London: Sheldon, 1979.

Edinger, Edward F. *The Sacred Psyche*, Toronto, Can: Inner City, 2004.

Elkins, D. N., L. J. Hedstrom, L. L. Hughes, J. A. Leaf, and C. Saunders, C. (1988). "Toward a Humanistic-phenomenological Spirituality." *Journal of Humanistic Psychology*, 28 (1988) 5–18.

Erickson, Millard J. *Christian Theology*. Grand rapids, MI: Baker, 1985.

Ferguson, Sinclair B. "Daniel." In *New Bible Commentary*, edited by D. A. Carson et al., 745–63. Nottingham, UK: IVP, 2011.

Friberg, Timothy, Barbara Friberg, and Neva F. Miller. *Analytical Lexicon of the Greek New Testament*. Crewe, UK: Trafford, 2005.

Gibb, H. A. R. "Islam." In *The Concise Encyclopaedia of Living Faiths*, edited by R. C. Zaehner, 166–99. London: Hutchinson, 1977.

Gibson, John C. L. *Genesis Volume 1*. Edinburgh: Saint Andrew, 1981.

———. *Genesis, Volume 11*. Edinburgh: Saint Andrew, 1982.

Grant, Michael. *The History of Ancient Israel*. London: Weidenfeld & Nicolson, 1984.

Hamilton, James M. "Still Sola Scripture: An Evangelical View of Scripture." In *The Sacred Texts: Excavating the Texts, Exploring the Interpretations, and Engaging in the Theologies of the Christian Scriptures*, edited by M. Bird and M. Pahl. Gorglas Précis Portfolios7. Piscatway: Gorglas, 2010.

Harris, Sam. "Free Will." In *50 Philosophy Classics: Thinking, Being, Acting, Seeing—Profound Insights and Powerful Thinking from Fifty Key Books*, edited by Tom Butler-Bowdon, 114–8. London: Nicholas Brealey, 2013

Hawkins, Stephen, and Leonard Mlodinow. *The Grand Design; New Answers to the Ultimate Questions of Life*. London: Bantam, 2010.

Hick, John. *Arguments for the Existence of God*. New York: Herber & Herber, 1971.

Heiler, F. *Erscheinungsformen und Wesen der Religion*. Stuttgart: Köhlhammer Verlag, 1961.

Hiebert, R. J. V. "Amos, Theology of." In *Baker's Evangelical Dictionary of Biblical Theology*, edited by W. A. Elwell. Grand Rapids, Mich: Baker, 1996.

Howse, Christopher. "The Meaning of the 'Name' of God." *Daily Telegraph*, UK, 37, published 18th June, 2016.

James, John. *Haggai, Zechariah and Malachi*. Leicester, UK: Crossway, 1996.

Joyner, Donald. *The Twelfth Journey*. Mustang, Oklahoma: Tate, 2013.

Keener, Craig S. *Miracles*. Grand Rapids, Mich: Baker Academic, 2011.

Kidner, Derek. "Isaiah." In *New Bible Commentary*, edited by D. A. Carson et al., 629–70. Nottingham, UK: IVP, 2011.

Knight, G. A. F. *The Psalms, Volume* 2. Edinburgh: Saint Andrew, 1983.

Koenig, Harold G. *The Healing Power of Faith*. New York: Simon and Schuster, 2001.

———. "A commentary: The Role of Religion and Spirituality at the End of Life." *The Gerontologist*, 42 (2002) 20–3.

Longman, Tremper, and Raymond B. Dillard, *An Introduction to the Old Testament*. Nottingham, UK: IVP, 2007.

Lowis, Michael J. *The Gospel Miracles: What Really Happened?* Eugene, OR: Resource, 2014.

Mark, Joshua J. *Burial Definition*. (Accessed December, 2016) http://www.ancient.eu/burial/.

———. *Ancient Egyptian Religion*. (January, 2016). http://www.ancient.eu/image/3428/.

McCartney, Dan, and Charles Clayton. *Let the Reader Understand: A Guide to Interpreting and Applying the Bible* (2nd ed). Phillipsburg, NJ: P & R, 2002.

McCasland, S. V., and G. E. Cairns. *Religions of the World*. New York: Random House, 1969.

McClellan, Matt. "Abraham and the Chronology of Ancient Mesopotamia." (October, 2012). https://answersingenesis.org/bible-timeline/abraham-and-the-chronology-of-ancient-mesopotamia/.

McConville, Gordon. "Jeremiah." In *New Bible Commentary*, edited by D. A. Carson et al., 671–708. Nottingham, UK: IVP, 2011.

———. "Lamentations." In *New Bible Commentary*, edited by D. A. Carson et al., 709–15. Nottingham, UK: IVP, 2011.

McDonald, D. A., L. Le Clair, C. J. Holland, A. Alter, and H. L. Friedman. "A Survey of Measures of Transpersonal Constructs." *Journal of Transpersonal Psychology*, 27 (1995) 171–231.

McGregor, L. John. "Ezekiel." In *New Bible Commentary*, edited by D. A. Carson et al., 716–44. Nottingham, UK: IVP, 2011.

McKim, D. K. *Historical Handbook of Major Biblical Interpreters*. Downers Grove IL: IVP, 1998.

McQuilkin, Robertson. *Understanding and Applying the Bible*. Chicago ILL: Moody, 2009.

Naylor, Peter J. "Numbers." In *New Bible Commentary*, edited by D. A. Carson et al., 158–97. Nottingham, UK: IVP, 2011.

Norris, R. A. "Antiochene Interpretation." In *A Dictionary of Biblical Interpretation*, edited by R. J. Coggins and J. L. Holden, 29–32. London: SCM, 1990.

Osborne, Grant R. *The Hermeneutical Spiral.* Downers Grove, IL, IVP Academic, 2006.

Parrinder, Geoffrey. *Asian Religions.* London: Sheldon, 1968.

Prabhavananda, Swami, and Christopher Isherwood, Christopher (Trans). *Bhagavad-Gita.* London: Phoenix House, 1972.

Ringgren, H., and A. V. Ström. *Religions of Mankind—Yesterday and Today.* London: Oliver & Boyd, 1967.

Roach, John. *Ancient Figurines Found—From First Modern Humans?* (December, 2003). http://news.nationalgeographic.com/news/2003/12/1217_031217_modernhumans.html.

Söderblom, N. *Das Werdeen des Gottesglaubens.* Leipzig: J. C. Hindrichssche Buchhandlung, 1916.

Stallard, M. "Literary interpretation: The Key to Understanding the Bible." *Journal of Ministry and Theology*, 4 (2000) 14–55.

Than, Ker. "Neanderthal Burials." (December 2013). http://news.nationalgeographic.com/news/2013/12/131216-la-chapelle-neanderthal-burials-graves.

Van der Leeuw, G., & Bleeker, C. J. *De Godsdiensten der Wereld.* Amsterdam: Meulenhoff, 1955.

Walton, John H. "Deuteronomy: An Exposition of the Spirit of the Law." *Grace Theological Journal*, 8 (1987) 213–25.

Wenham, G. J. "Genesis." In *New Bible Commentary*, edited by D. A. Carson et al., 55–91. Nottingham, UK: IVP, 2011.

Wilson, Ian. "Divine presence in Deuteronomy." *Tyndale Bulletin*, 42 (1992) 403–7.

Wright, C. J. H. *The Mission of God.* Downers Grove, Il, IVP, 2006.

Wright, J. Stafford. *Psalms.* London: Scripture Union, 1982.

Lightning Source UK Ltd.
Milton Keynes UK
UKOW01f1055011117
312000UK00007B/800/P